RELEASING THE SPIRIT

RANDY SHANKLE

Whitaker House

RELEASING THE SPIRIT

Randy Shankle
P.O. Box 8320
Marshall, TX 75671

ISBN: 0-88368-461-6
Printed in the United States of America
Copyright © 1987 by Randy Shankle

Whitaker House
580 Pittsburgh Street
Springdale, PA 15144

CONTENTS

Introduction
PART I: The *Merismos* of the Spirit and Soul
1   "Dividing Asunder" of Spirit and Soul   11
2   The Smoking Furnace and Burning Lamp   19
3   A House Diveded Against Itself   31

PART II: The Realm of the Soul
4   "*Psuche* Souffle"   45
5   Saving of the Soul   63
6   The Super Soul   74
7   The Oversoul   86
8   Metamorphosis of the Mind   97
9   Gethsemane: The Wine Press   115
10 Understanding the *Psuche* Realm   134
11 Controlling the Soul   152
12 Hearing Through Waiting   171
13 The Waiting of the Soul   184

PART III: The Uniting of the Heart
14 The Divided Heart   203
15 The Release of the Spirit   216
16 Beauty in Brokenness   227

INTRODUCTION

In this book, there are teachings that probably will touch some "golden calves" of various readers, because this revelation from the Holy Spirit gets into the ramifications of the soul, into "soulish displays" and the "lifestyles of the self."

The reader needs to understand that the soul does not want to be changed, not even to conform to the image of Christ. The spirit man may understand the need to change, but the soul — which has been "programmed" from birth with the social, cultural, and environmental thought patterns and habits of behavior of the natural world — will fight to maintain the status quo. Instinctive survival mechanisms are triggered by any attempt to change body or soul habits just the same as if a person actually was under a physical attack. The result is inner conflict, or the feeling of fighting oneself. It may seem like trying to paddle a boat upstream against the current.

Also, I will be explaining areas of ministry that seem to deal with other men and women of God, but I am *not* talking about them personally. I am simply talking about the way of the soul. I do not want, nor do I intend, to criticize any ministry or any man or woman of God. Please do not interpret any comments that seem to fit those you know or have heard of as personal slander. This book deals with the soulish realm, which will automatically identify all of us.

The ramifications of the soul are many and varied and, although I do not intend for this book to be criticism, it necessarily will be, but in the form of exposure, because nothing is hidden from God. All things are naked and open to Him. What the *merismos* revelation will do is use the Word of God to expose more and more of you to yourself. In the concept of a physician, Christ has placed within me a two-edged sword which will do some "operating" on you — if you let it. The sword will not, however, take a big chunk out of you all at once. It will penetrate deeper and deeper into the areas where darkness lies, areas where you do not know what is there, and areas where you do not know why you acted as you did. The sword will bring an incision and expose the reality.

> **The spirit of man is the candle of the Lord,**
> **searching all the inward parts of the belly.**
> **Proverbs 20:27**

That verse means that the spirit is the flashlight of God which turns light on all the inward parts of a man and causes deep to call unto deep. The hidden mysteries of Jesus Christ are going to begin to be called forth by your spirit. He will call for the deep things of your spirit and of your soul, things that have been hidden away for years and represent the way you are. Products of your environment, your culture, or your exposure to somebody or something and products of pain, rejection, or misunderstanding have formed your personality. You are programmed so that you respond the same way to any stimuli that appears the same as the original, even if it is actually very different.

You have become predictable to the devil, if not to your immediate family and friends. As long as you operate in the natural, soulish realm, you are vulnerable to satanic temptations, attacks, and guidances. Only when your spirit man is fully in charge is Satan at a loss, because he has no understanding or ability to predict the actions of a truly "spiritual" man or woman. That is why the devil was so badly fooled about Jesus, even to the extent of thinking that if His body was killed, it would be the end of Him on Earth.

What we are going to do is use the engrafted Word, the incorruptible seed, to take out of you the corruptible mentality and replace it with God's incorruptible mentality. Those things that have kept your spirit from soaring, from being lifted up to the heavenly realm, will be taken out. Everything that has kept you from experiencing the spiritual dimension of Christ will be exposed through this teaching.

It is time that the Body of Christ steps over into a brand new dimension, into God's light, walking in the light as He is in the light (1 John 1:7). We can move over into that realm and experience the total freedom that comes when the spirit man dominates and controls the lifestyle, when the soul and body are brought into subjection, and where, at no time, is there resistance to the pure flow of the Holy Spirit. That freedom is available, but you have to work in the Word of God to get there.

The *merismos* teaching is another manifestation of the Holy Spirit to the Body of Christ, another wave of His power, and one day, that "wave" will become a "way," a way of life.

There still are a lot of things that I do not know about all this; but, what I do know, *I know.* What I do not know, I am going to learn. As I learn, I adapt my new knowledge into the revelation realm of God, and it becomes an absolute. The Word of God is an absolute. Jesus Christ is absolute. His entire message was an absolute. He preached, "You are either for me or against me. You are either this or that." (Luke 11:23.)

We must let the Word of God become the absolute in our lives. When the Word speaks, that must settle the issue.

A Possible Pitfall

A possible pitfall of this teaching is the extreme to which people can take it. There are always those who carry any teaching to the extreme. It would be an extreme position of the *merismos* teaching to not make a move without "hearing from God." Some people get weird with this. They wait to hear from God which tie to put on, what color of dress to wear, whether to eat chicken or roast beef for dinner. They won't go to the grocery store until God speaks to them.

The whole reason for saving the soul is so that he can move with God. God does not have to *tell* me to go to church, pay my tithes, or do those things that are plainly shown in His Word. Once the soul gets saved, he knows the will of God in certain areas. **Be ye transformed . . . that ye may prove what is that good, and acceptable, and perfect, will of God** (Rom. 12:2).

I now know, without a "special revelation" or "a word from God," that I am to read my Bible and pray. My soul has been saved and transformed to know that *is* the will of God. Now my soul can make the decisions of a determined will. He purposes to pray and to seek God. **Bless the Lord, O my** *soul*: **and** *all* **that is within me . . .** (Ps. 103:1) denotes all of the soulish realm. Bless the Lord with my mind, will, and emotions. I don't have to wait for the spirit man to tell the soul to bless and worship God. He now knows that it is the will of God. So, let's don't get "flaky" with this teaching.

PART I
THE *MERISMOS* OF THE
SPIRIT AND SOUL

1
"DIVIDING ASUNDER" OF SPIRIT AND SOUL

Merismos is the act of making a distinction between the spirit, the soul, and the body of man. Now, this separation is only for the purpose of clarification and does not mean that the spirit, soul, and body are actually detached from one another. *Merismos* means taking all the facets of a man and separating them into the categories of spirit, soul, and body, then breaking down each of these areas into further components for revelation and clarity in order that we may have a greater understanding of man. *Merismos* is the Greek word translated "dividing asunder" in Hebrews 4:12.

For the word of God is quick, and powerful, and sharper than any two-edged sword, piercing even to the dividing asunder of soul and spirit, and of the joints and marrow, and is a discerner of the thoughts and intents of the heart.

Neither is there any creature that is not manifest in his sight: but all things are naked and opened unto the eyes of him with whom we have to do.

Hebrews 4:12,13

This word *merismos* comes from two other Greek root words: *merizo*, which means "to part, to apportion, to disunite, to separate," and *meros*, which means "to

11

get as a section or allotment, a division, or share." Therefore, *merismos* means "a separation or distinction made between separate parts." The only other time the word is used in the Bible is in Hebrews 2:4:

> **God also bearing them witness, both with signs and wonders, and with divers miracles, and gifts of the Holy Ghost, according to his own will.**

The word translated "gifts" is *merismos* in the Greek original text, the *merismos* of the Holy Ghost, or the "dividing of His manifestations (gifts) into the various parts of the Body of Christ." Every one of the ministries in the Spirit of God's operation is distinct from the others. In other words, each gift has a clarification or separate appearance so that we can know what God wants to do in the Body of Christ; and, when He does it, we are able to find out what He is doing.

The Word separates the soul and spirit of a man. The *only* thing that can is the Word. Psychologists have tried it, psychiatrists have tried it, doctors have tried it, everybody else has tried it. The best the world has come up with is that man is dualistic: soul and body, but he is not. Man is spirit, soul, and body (1 Thess. 5:23). Only the Word can take a man's soulish realm and spirit realm, separate and segregate them into certain areas, and define them.

Again, let me say that we are talking about a separation for clarification. I am not referring to these areas becoming detached from one another. In other words, God does not "divide" the spirit and soul and send them in opposite directions. The Word brings revelation into these realms so that we can see clearly which one we have operated in, even in our Christian lives: spiritual, soulish, or carnal (the realm of the body or the flesh).

I am sorry to say that, for many years, I operated in Christianity in the soulish realm. I adapted the spiritual principles of God to the soulish realm, and that very thing is going on today in the majority of Christians and Christian ministries. One of the major confusions coming into the Body — and most Christians are totally unaware of it — is that spirit men (*pneumatikos*) and soul men (*psuchikos*) are appearing on the same platforms and teaching identical principles.

One man teaching the power of positive faith and confession is teaching from the vantage point of spiritual principles. Another man is teaching the same principles from the world of the soul, yet the Body has not made a distinction. In most cases, members of the Body have embraced both teachings without discernment; or, because of recognizing one realm as soulish, have thrown out God's spiritual principles along with the soulish teachings.

Now, I am *into* the faith message. I operate in the faith of God, so I am not talking against that message. What I am talking about are those who are adapting the principles of the Word *to* their lives without having a real work of the Spirit of God *in* their lives. They are channeling the principles of the Spirit into the soulish realm. Everything sounds like the Spirit, but it is wrong. It is of the soul and not of the spirit. It is learned knowledge, or principles applied through the mind, not Spirit-revealed. That which is of the flesh is flesh.

We are having a merging back into the Body of Christ of spiritual principles that have been taught to the world. The world's system is picking them up and learning them and using the same phraseology. Now the principles are being taught on the same platform, at the same pulpit, sometimes in week-long seminars, but filtered through two systems — the spiritual and the natural. And most Christians do not even know it.

You can be born again, Spirit-filled, talk in tongues, and still spend ninety percent of your life in the soulish realm. You can teach and minister from the soulish realm with no life, no power, and no freedom, for each realm reproduces "after its own kind."

It is the spirit that quickeneth; the flesh profiteth nothing: the words that I speak unto you, they are spirit, and they are life.

John 6:63

The first stage of the *merismos* is "revelation for illumination." God brings the revelation that He wants to separate your spirit and soul. The second stage is "separation for clarification." In this stage, He will clarify the aspects of the soul — the mind, will, and emotions — and the various aspects of each of these soulish areas. After He separates and deals with the soul, then He brings it back into union with the spirit, which is the third stage, "unification for cooperation."

Three Areas of Separation

The three major areas that *merismos* pertains to in Hebrews 4:12 are: *spirit and soul, joints and marrow, and thoughts and intents of the heart*. These are the areas where the Word of God needs to separate our lives.

If you stay in the Word long enough, it will take your *spirit and soul* and separate them, clarifying the different lifestyles of each because the Word is sharper than a two-edged sword. God will show you how much time you really spend operating from the soulish realm.

Once He separates one aspect from the rest, He will deal with it. We use the phrase, "I got dealt with." There are ways that the Word of God deals with the soul man and removes from him the strengths of arrogance, haughtiness, opinions, pride, boastings, dominance, pushiness — all of those things that man believes make up a "hot-rod" lifestyle. God's dealings will take all of that out of the soul man, then bring him back into submission.

The soul man goes out looking like superman, then comes back crawling on his knees saying, "Will you receive me?" He comes back into submission to the spirit, and from that moment on, a person becomes *pneumatikos*, spirit-ruled. He begins to operate as a spirit being. After this separation, he will check everything he does with Christ, the Head. He will not check in with his soul or allow the soul man to dictate his lifestyle anymore. This condition is a beautiful and attainable goal.

The *joints and marrow* are areas where prophetic revelation is going on in the earth today. Marrow is the jelly-like substance within the bones that reproduces the blood — and the life of the body is in the blood. The marrow also carries the nutrients from one joint to another for the health and growth of the bone. The nutrients are what make the bones strong. When a joint is dislocated, the marrow dries up. This picture of the human body is a description of the Body of Christ as well.

When a bone is out of joint or in the wrong place in the Body, the marrow will not flow. Independent ministries — and I was one of them — did what they were supposed to in the 60s and 70s. But now the cloud of the Holy Spirit has moved on to another place. I do not mean, of course, that these ministries are to end. From the beginning, God has always had one man that He has dealt with as the forerunner of something He is doing. The move of the Holy Spirit now is not to get rid of the one-man ministry but to incorporate that ministry into the right place in the Body of Christ, to get each "bone" set properly into the right "joint" so His marrow can flow freely.

Jesus is going back to church. He shared with me about the joints and marrow in a vision (related in tapes called the "Zion Series," available from ministry headquarters) in which He took the "joints and marrow" analogy and prophesied where the Body of Christ is out of joint. What happens when someone in the Body gets out of joint? The marrow dries up so that what he or she is trying to do no longer brings life. Whenever you want to see where the move of God is, check out the "marrow," and you will see whether a ministry is in or out of joint.

What Jesus said He was going to do was to dislocate me, then relocate me, and He did that in my life. When He spoke to me about this, Randy Shankle Ministries, Inc. had six or eight staff members.

Jesus said, "I want you to shut it down. It's all over with. RSM is all over with." And I let Him do it.

I walked out of my office and told the staff, "It's all over with. You can go home. The cloud has moved on. This move of God has come to an end." I told my chief administrator, "It's all over with, brother. You can go get yourself a job."

Startled, he looked at me and asked, "Go get a job?"

I said, "Go get yourself a job. I'm shutting this thing down and going to church."

He got a job for about a year. Then, when I relocated and did what Jesus told me to do, I called him back and said, "Now brother, it's time." He rejoined me in the ministry and, boy, has he been an asset! He is a bishop of the church now and one of the most incredible assets I have ever seen in the Body of Christ. He is hooked up right this time.

When I walked out and got ready to lock the door, I looked at all that land and the office. The staff was gone. The equipment was gone. The desks and furniture were gone. I sat and looked at everything and started to cry. Fourteen years of a vision were gone, but I relocated properly. I had to realize that the cloud of the Lord that we had been following in the 60s and 70s had moved on into the distance. I said, "Lord, I don't want to be foolish. I want to stay in the flow of the Holy Spirit."

I made my decision, and it was the right decision. Jesus is going back to church, and that is what I did. I was out of joint. I had to get dislocated and relocated. A lot of people go from one church to another trying to find a great move of God somewhere, but they have no marrow. They are not reproducing life, just looking for it. They will never reproduce life until they get located in a body that flows with life.

Those that be planted in the house of the Lord shall flourish in the courts of our God.

Psalm 92:13

You will never flourish in the courts (in ministry) until you get planted in the House of the Lord. The Holy Spirit is singing a brand new song. You might as well pick up on the tune. If you don't, in two or three years, you'll be prehistoric. I am not speaking in

17

condemnation, just telling you honestly. When I find out where the drift is, I get in on the flow. If you want to get in on the flow, you have to get in the know. This is the dividing of the joints and marrow which is going on today in the Church.

The *thoughts and intents of the heart* are two different things. How often have you seen someone say one thing and do another? The intents of his heart may be in line with the Word of God, but his behavior may be 180 degrees different because his soul thoughts are stronger. The two-edged sword of the Word will separate these two aspects of a person and illuminate the fact that they are not in alignment. Non-alignment causes double-mindedness, or conflict between spirit and flesh or spirit and soul.

2

THE SMOKING FURNACE
AND BURNING LAMP

Do you know why many Christians became so excited about faith and confession in the 60s and 70s? They were sure that this teaching was going to show them how to experience God in their lives. Some of you are still sure of it. It is true that you have to have faith to please God at all, and it is true that you will not receive without believing God. The Bible says in Genesis 15:6, **And he** (Abraham) **believed in the Lord; and he counted it to him for righteousness.**

We need to take this basic teaching a step farther. Faith is of the spirit realm. If the soul man and not the spirit man is in control of your life, is that condition going to hinder the force of faith? Yes! Unbelief is of the soulish realm, and if it can get into the heart of a man, it will negate or block the force of God — for faith is of the spirit. (See Chapter 14, "The Divided Heart.") Let's look at Abraham when God began to talk about "cutting a covenant" with him and giving him a son.

And he said unto him, I am the Lord that brought thee out of Ur of the Chaldees, to give thee this land to inherit it.
And he (Abraham) **said, Lord God, whereby shall I know that I shall inherit it?**

Genesis 15:7,8

Look closely at what Abraham is saying: "How will I know that I will come into my inheritance? How will

19

I know for sure that I will receive what You have promised me? Can You give me some understanding of how I will know that?"

Does that seem like a question out of the Body of Christ? "How can I really know how to experience what God has for me, to walk in His provision, and to experience what He did for me on Calvary? How can I really do it?"

We see through the story of Abraham that God did not leave it all just hanging on faith. He gave Abraham faith *and* something else, and He gives us faith *and* something else. God said to Abraham, "I am going to show you the revelation of the covenant." We have not understood our covenant relationship with God. We have not gotten the revelation of this. Honestly, we haven't. As you read the rest of the experience of Abraham with the covenant of God, you will see what I am talking about.

> **And he said unto him, (Abraham) Take me an heifer of three years old, and a she goat of three years old, and a ram of three years old, and a turtledove, and a young pigeon.**
>
> **And he took unto him all these, and divided them in the midst, and laid each piece one against another: but the birds divided he not.**
>
> **Genesis 15:9,10**

Before he divided them, were they one piece? Yes! Before he took the goat, ram, and heifer and divided them, they were each one animal. When he laid them out, there were two pieces of each animal. Each of the animals was one piece, and it became two pieces. Read closely. That is the purpose of the sacrifice. This is God cutting the covenant in reality.

20

And when the fowls came down upon the carcases, Abram drove them away.

Genesis 15:11

Abraham drove the fowls of prey away, not God. When you go through a *merismos* of the Lord, the "fowls" come, and it is up to you to get rid of them. Every Christian who is at all teachable has gone through lots of *merismos* experiences and doesn't know it. Once you find out what this experience is, you can learn to better cooperate with what God is doing. Every time you are dealt with by God, there is a way to understand how to cooperate with Him properly so that you can inherit the provisions of the covenant. The purpose of a *merismos* is to get you into a position to experience and inherit the provisions of God's covenant with man.

There is something that will take place each time God wants you to experience the next dimension of your life or of His Word. You will experience a *merismos* before you receive. Haven't you heard the old statement, "The moment I began to believe God for my health, I got sick?" You'd better believe it. The moment you began to believe God for your finances, things got worse. It always works that way, because *immediately the fowls come.*

Satan cometh immediately and taketh away the word (Mark 4:15) to keep it from *merismosing* you and getting you to the place where you can experience your inheritance. When the "fowls" come in to defer the purpose of God and throw you a decoy, if you go after it, you will get away from the blessing. You will come out of the experience with a wrong way of thinking and a wrong way of believing. You will not inherit, but if you drive the fowls away during this time, the Word

21

can keep on separating and laying the pieces, divided by the sword of the Lord, one against another for a purpose.

> And when the sun was going down, a deep sleep fell upon Abram; and, lo, an horror of great darkness fell upon him.

> And he said unto Abram, Know of a surety that thy seed shall be a stranger in a land that is not theirs, and shall serve them; and they shall afflict them four hundred years. (Here God began to prophesy of the Israelite's captivity in Egypt and of His promised deliverance.)

> And it came to pass, that, when the sun went down, and it was dark, behold a smoking furnace, and a burning lamp that passed between those pieces.

> Genesis 15:12,13,17

In the midst of darkness, Abraham looked up and saw something. Who is the *Merismos* Man? Who is the Covenant Man? His name is Jesus. Abraham saw the same thing that the writer of Hebrews saw. He was in darkness and those pieces of the animals were cut in the center and laid one on one side and one on the other, then something started walking between them. On one hand, Abraham saw a burning lamp and, on the other hand, a smoking furnace. He saw a cloud and fire, or light. The cloud and fire were going between those pieces. What does the smoking furnace represent? What does the cloud represent? They represent Jesus, His presence, the *shekinah* glory.

The presence of God, the glory of God through Jesus Christ, came to seal the covenant during that hour. This was a sacred moment: Almighty God became partner with man in a covenant, and Jesus, the Covenant Man, passing between those pieces, was bringing the presence and the glory of God. He was bringing the lamp. Psalm 119:105 says, **Thy Word is a lamp unto my feet, and a light unto my path.** The presence and glory of God was the Spirit and the Word together, walking between the pieces of that covenant so that Abraham could experience his inheritance. Jesus brought light for revelation of the two parts of the covenant sacrifices.

Are we to offer up our bodies to Him as a living sacrifice? Yes. Romans 12:1 says so. When we do, He will walk between the divided parts of our bodies with His Word and Spirit and show us how to inherit the promises. He will bring light into the realm of the spirit man and into the soulish realm and will bring the Word to expose both areas. He will bring His presence, or glory, and show us which aspects of our beings will bring glory to Him and which will not. That is called "the covenant."

The reason we have not really participated in the true covenant of God is that we do not want to use the terminology. The covenant sign was the circumcision of the male flesh. God wants to cut something out of our hearts. Most Christians have no idea why God cut the foreskin of the male. The reason was that the power of reproduction of life is in the male. God cuts away the flesh so that, when the power of reproduction comes forth, it will not be touched with flesh in any area. No flesh will have anything to do with the reproduction. Circumcision was a shadow, or a picture, in the natural world of God's purpose and actions in the realm of the spirit.

23

One of the Greek words for "word" is *sperma*. God's Word is the seed of reproduction. When it comes forth, it reproduces life — the new birth, healing, deliverance, etc. His Word will not come forth in power or reproduction unless the flesh is cut away and nothing touches or mingles with it. The Word comes out in the purity of spirit with no impurities, no soulish overtones, no soulish inclinations, no soulish adding to prophecy or taking away from it, nothing that does not reproduce spirit life.

Have you ever been in a service where someone got up and prophesied out of his or her mentality, out of the soul? Did you feel that "yucky" feeling in the atmosphere? Flesh touched the gift of prophecy and perverted the purity of it. It will not bring forth a child. It will be aborted. No one received life from that word. When God's Word constantly is tampered with mentally and through the soulish realm, you are not going to receive what you want from God.

God said to Abraham, "I'll show you a surety, or how to receive. I am going to give you an absolute surety that you and your seed will receive from Me. The surety is that I am going to show you how to cut away that which would negate the force of My promises in your life. And it is your soul."

He divided the sacrifice which was one (the heart) and showed two pieces (spirit and soul). In Hebrews, we read that **the word of God is quick, and powerful, and sharper than any two-edged sword, piercing even to the dividing asunder of soul and spirit** (Heb. 4:12a). God lays out those two pieces and shows us how the soul is negating the spirit.

Every time God wants to do something, the soul says, "Well, I don't know if it's for me." Flesh just tampered with the zoe, the life of the Word.

"It passed away; it's not for today." "Not everybody gets it; not everybody *should* get it; it's not God's will for everyone to get it." Every word like that is a soulish overtone of religious tradition, and every bit of that stuff needs to be circumcised from your heart, or you will never inherit. Religion, tradition, denominationalism — all of that needs to be circumcised, but not to start another religion, tradition, or denomination! It needs to be cut off from the Body to keep the Word pure and unadulterated.

The purpose of the *merismos* is to take each life and separate it so that the covenant of God and His provision in our lives can be experienced more readily and a whole lot faster than in the past.

Take another look at Abraham's life. Immediately after God revealed this to him, he dropped back into the soulish realm.

> Now Sarai Abram's wife bare him no children: and she had a handmaid, an Egyptian, whose name was Hagar.

> And Sarai said unto Abram, Behold now, the Lord hath restrained me from bearing: I pray thee, go in unto my maid; it may be that I may obtain children by her. And Abram hearkened to the voice of Sarai.

> And Sarai, Abram's wife, took Hagar her maid the Egyptian, after Abram had dwelt ten years in the land of Canaan, and gave her to her husband Abram to be his wife.

> Genesis 16:1-3

That sounded like a nice, rational, reasonable solution to God's promise. "Since I cannot have it and cannot get it, we'll just find somebody else. Go to my handmaiden." So Abraham went back to the world. He took the Egyptian. **Woe to them that go down to Egypt for help** (Isa. 31:1). Just because circumstances look as if you are not getting the promise, don't go to the world to get it by some other means. If you don't know how to get it from God, learn how. Don't substitute secondary means. There is no "Plan B" to this thing. Stay in there and learn how to receive what God promised you. Don't blame Him and His Word. Find out where you are wrong. Abraham went down to Hagar, to "Egypt," to find the fulfillment of the promise, and the world gave it to him.

> **And he went in unto Hagar, and she conceived: and when she saw that she had conceived, her mistress was despised in her eyes.**
>
> **Genesis 16:4**

Anytime you go the way of the soul, it will despise your spirit every time. The soul man will mock at your ignorance and your compromise and do nothing but condemn you.

> **And Sarai said unto Abram, My wrong be upon thee: I have given my maid into thy bosom; and when she saw that she had conceived, I was despised in her eyes: the Lord judge between me and thee.**
>
> **But Abram said unto Sarai, Behold, thy maid is in thy hand; do to her as it pleaseth thee. And when Sarai dealt hardly with her, she fled from her face.** (Hagar means "to take flight or flee," so that's what she did. And, when things get rough, the soul flees.)

And the angel of the Lord found her by a fountain of water in the wilderness, by the fountain in the way to Shur.

And he said, Hagar, Sarai's maid, whence camest thou? and whither wilt thou go? And she said, I flee from the face of my mistress Sarai.

And the angel of the Lord said unto her, Return to thy mistress, and submit thyself under her hands.

And the angel of the Lord said unto her, I will multiply thy seed exceedingly, that it shall not be numbered for multitude.

And the angel of the Lord said unto her, Behold, thou art with child, and shalt bear a son, and shalt call his name Ishmael; because the Lord hath heard thy affliction.

And he will be a wild man; his hand will be against every man, and every man's hand against him; and he shall dwell in the presence of all his brethren.

Genesis 16:5-12

Does this happen today? Absolutely! The soul and spirit dwell together in the same house in warfare. The soul is called a "wild man" and, until he is dealt with, is extremely arrogant. Jeremiah uses the same Hebrew word, but it is translated "wild ass." It describes a donkey, stubborn, rebellious, disobedient, and self-willed. That nature is a part of your life until it is dealt with.

You may say, "No, that's not right. When I got born again, I got a new nature."

Yes, you received a new nature, but you didn't get a change of life. You still have *zoe* life and *psuche* life. Your personality did not pass away. We do not have a dualistic nature, but we do have two kinds of life. Before Adam sinned, he had the divine nature of God, but he also had the life of the spirit and the life of the soul. He was created a *nephesh*, a "living soul." After he sinned, he lost the zoe life of the spirit but kept his own *psuche* (soul) life. He also exchanged the divine nature for a sin nature.

When Jesus came, He said, **I am come that they might have life, and that they might have it more abundantly** (John 10:10b). "Life" in this verse is *zoe*, which means that man did not have it, but Jesus got it back for us. He said, **I lay down my life** (John 10:15): *psuche*, self-life. To get the *zoe* back, Jesus had to give up his self-life. What Adam lost was given back to us by Calvary. Jesus bore the sin nature so that we could have the divine nature. Now we can be partakers of the divine nature. You have been given back *zoe*; however, it is still living with the life of self in your body. The war is not between the sin nature and the divine nature. The war is between the choice of living your life or God's life. Unless you get the soul man dealt with, he will do what the Word of God said not to do. He will always go to the Tree of Knowledge of Good and Evil.

When Satan appeared to Adam and Eve in the garden, what area or realm of man did he tempt? He tempted the soulish realm, or the mind, will, and emotions: the area of choice. Satan asked Adam and Eve to make a choice. What is incredible is that God already had warned them not to choose that tree, but they chose independently of God's will. The independent lifestyle is *psuche* — "I'll do what *I* want to do."

Satan threw man a curve and presented two major doctrines that are still in the earth: "You shall be as gods" and "You shall not die." We recognize these today as *humanism* and *reincarnation*. Religion can be good in man's eyes, but it has too many "0's" — good, not God. It will kill you if you partake of that trash. There is no life in *either* good *or* evil in the soul realm. When Satan has man operating on "Isaac and Ishmael" principles, he constantly leads him to the Tree of Knowledge of Good and Evil, and we forget that it is the knowledge of good *and* evil.

Christians will not go out and rob and kill (partake of the knowledge of evil), but they will go to the "knowledge of good," yet it is the same tree! They do not surrender their lives to God's life and ask Him what He wants done. They tell God where they are going and what they are doing and ask Him to bless it. That is soulish and is going to be death to them.

I learned this principle years ago. When I get an invitation to minister, I don't go to the Tree of Knowledge of Good and Evil, for in the day that I partake of it, I die. My soul may want to call and say, "How many are there? How much is the offering going to be? How long do I have to stay? How little do I have to do? The moment I am through preaching, can I leave the pulpit and go to my motel room?"

No! What I must do is get on my knees and say, "Jesus, You are the Head of the Church, and You are the Lord of my life. Now, do You want me to go?"

That choice brings me to the Tree of Life. I choose life. I renounce the choice of my soul that would go to something that sounds or looks good, something that is going to benefit me. One of the kinds of people God says *not* to put into the ministry is a novice. (1 Tim. 3:6)

Job 7:2 tells why: **As a servant earnestly desireth the shadow, and as an hireling looketh for the reward of his work.** Novices look for the shade and the wage: the least amount of work for the most amount of pay. Pulpits are full of them, "Untouchable Ministries, Inc."

You cannot experience God's best in your life unless you can tap the Spirit of God in any individual. The woman with the issue of blood got healing because she pressed in and touched the hem of His garment and *dunamis* (power) flowed out of Him. You have to make contact to get the power of the Spirit. The kind of contact we have had is from the pulpit to the pew, and that is not the way of the spirit. That is the way of the soul. That is a self-preservation technique. It is thinking of yourself more highly than you ought to think. It is separating the ministers from the people, with a mentality that says, "I don't have time to touch your life," or "I'm too important to touch your life," or whatever else the soulish mentality has been.

The entire teaching of Jesus is for us to give our lives. He told us to do it **even as the Son of man** (Who) **came not to be ministered unto, but to minister, and to give his life** *(psuche)* **a ransom for many** (Matt. 20:28). Apostles, prophets, evangelists, pastors, and teachers are not called to be ministered unto. Anyone with this attitude needs to get out of the ministry and get dealt with some more in order to have the right attitude and the right heart behind what is being done.

The word *ministry* means "to serve." The literal definition is "office, relief, service(-ing)." Jesus said that He is looking for servants — not like the Gentiles who like to be lords. Jesus did not come to make leaders but servants. As soon as you become a servant, you are a leader.

3

A HOUSE DIVIDED AGAINST ITSELF

Every house, every kingdom, every city that is divided against itself cannot stand. Did you get divided before or after you were born again? After! Before you were born again, your spirit man and soul man were in unity. The spirit man was spiritually dead, and the soul man had preeminence. Consequently, the body did whatever felt good. The only correction available was not through the spirit, which was unregenerate, but through soul training, which is ethics and morals.

You may have gone to church or your parents may have taught you to be "good." It does not matter how morally or ethically good you are, **ye must be born again** (John 3:7), and the moment you are born again, you become a "house divided against itself." You have operations of both the spirit and the soul, *pneumatikos* and *psuchikos* dealings. A war goes on to see which is going to win. Two natures are not involved, but two kinds of life are fighting. The soul man does not need a sin nature. He has a selfish lifestyle. He is not wanting to sin — he just wants his own way, his own life. It may not be wanting evil, but if it comes from the same tree, it produces death.

> **Then was brought unto him one possessed with a devil, blind, and dumb: and he healed him, insomuch that the blind and dumb both spake and saw.**

31

And all the people were amazed, and said, Is not this the Son of David?

But when the Pharisees heard it, they said, This fellow doth not cast out devils, but by Beelzebub the prince of the devils.

And Jesus knew their thoughts, and said unto them, Every kingdom divided against itself is brought to desolation; and every city or house divided against itself shall not stand.

And if Satan cast out Satan, he is divided against himself; how shall then his kingdom stand?

And if I by Beelzebub cast out devils, by whom do your children cast them out? therefore they shall be your judges.

But if I cast out devils by the Spirit of God, then the kingdom of God is come unto you.

Or else, how can one enter into a strong man's house, and spoil his goods, except he first bind the strong man? and then he will spoil his house.

Matthew 12:22-29

"Divided" in verse 25 is the word *merizo,* one of the root words for *merismos.* It simply means "a separation or a division." The plan of God is to get you reunited properly with your soul submitted to your spirit so that you won't fall. This teaching is evidently needed today, because many Christians are failing, frustrated, defeated, full of anxiety, depressed, and trying to *make* things work.

Perhaps you are trying to make a ministry for yourself, doing everything you know how and even imitating others — getting a mailing list, a newsletter, and a partner program. Perhaps it worked for others, but that does not mean the same thing will work for you. Many are trying to teach, preach, and prophesy, being frustrated the whole time because they can't get God to promote them. They are members out of joint and have not realized it. There is no marrow, no life. The problem is that they are being controlled by their souls. If the soul man dictates your lifestyle, you are a house divided against itself. Many Christians are blaming God for their own situations.

When God deals with us, He deals with our souls in order to take out of us a part of Hagar (to flee, flight). "Hagar" always leaves when the going gets tough. Here are some things that reflect the soul man's lack of character: lack of commitment, unfaithfulness, no reliability or dependability, no punctuality, inconsistency, and a general lack of the other characteristics that *are* reflected in a man's life after he has been dealt with in the *merismos* by Jesus.

The Isaac-Ishmael Principle

Jesus never did anything through a "Hagar" mentality. He was committed to everything He laid His hands on. He stayed with it until He changed it. Jesus said *That which is born of the flesh is flesh; and that which is born of the Spirit is spirit* (John 3:6). An *Ishmael* is that which is born of the flesh and conceived in the mind of man, but *Isaac* is that which is born of the Spirit. Jesus Himself was the real Son of Promise of whom Isaac was the natural shadow or type.

If God's people do not desist from their own labors, they do what Sarah and Abraham did: conceive an *Ishmael*. God told Abraham that *He* would give him a

33

son but, after a few years when it did not look as if it would come to pass, *they* conceived the answer in their own soulish ingenuity. We need to remember that Romans 4:20 and 21 place the responsibility on God both for the promise and for the performance.

Many Christians think that the promise is God's responsibility and the performance of that promise is their own responsibility. If God has promised you a church, let *Him* perform it. If God has promised you prosperity, let *Him* perform it. Forget all your ways of making it happen. Those are Ishmaels, not Isaacs.

For it is written, that Abraham had two sons, the one by a bondmaid, the other by a freewoman.

Galatians 4:22

What is the nature of the two sons? One was flesh and the other was spirit. One was a work of the flesh and the other a work of the spirit, waiting for the promise and the fulfillment of God. God promises to bless you, and the soul says, "Yeah, and it will be here by midnight tomorrow. I'll see to that." God says, "I've opened a door for you," and your soul says, "Yeah!" Then you push against the door until it gives. You get on the phone and call all the men of God you know. You pass out your card and promote yourself. Jesus had the best card that you can have. He had a "John the Baptist." Every man has his "John the Baptist." He is the preceder of the way. The soul man doesn't wait for John the Baptist. He wants to create his own way. "Ishmaels," wild men, are rebellious and disobedient to God's order and purpose. They are in opposition to themselves and do not even know it.

But he who was of the bondwoman was born after the flesh . . . (Gal. 4:23). Does that refer only to natural

34

birth? No, it also means ideas, views, concepts, and programs born of the flesh. You are born from your mother's womb, which is flesh, but you must also be born after the Spirit; yet many born of the Spirit continue to reproduce a lot of things after the flesh.

We have a statement in our local body, "Raise your own babies!" When people come up with great ideas for us to do, I tell them, "Not us, you!" What has God told you to do? Don't bring it to me wanting me to raise your child. Take your own child, and we'll see if it was of God or not. "Ishmaels" come out of the soulish realm, not the spirit. They are born *after the flesh*, which means by man's own intelligence, creativity, ideas, views, and concepts. An Ishmael is the product (son) of reasonings, logic, and imaginations.

Paul said that an Ishmael **gendereth to bondage** (Gal. 4:24). That means: You conceive the idea, you pay for it. But what God promised, *He* is able also to perform. Ishmaels are costly. They bring financial and emotional bondage.

But he of the free woman was by promise *(Gal. 4:23b). Let me give you the Word of God that is for the spirit and corrects the soul. The Word always speaks to both the spirit and soul instantly.*

> **He staggered not at the promise of God through unbelief; but was strong in faith, giving glory to God;**
> **And being fully persuaded that, what he had promised, he was able also to perform.**
>
> **Romans 4:20,21**

What God has promised, you do not have to perform. He will. Your struggle ends where His Spirit begins. We cease from our own labors. If God promises you a ministry, then let Him perform it. You don't have to create it. No push, no pump, no pull. All of this is soulish activity, trying to get it done. **He which hath begun a good work in you will perform it** (Phil. 1:6). My faith is in what He said and what He will do. I enter into my rest and however long it takes for Him to do what He said — fine, but I know it will be done. In the meantime, I am going to enjoy the rest that is mine. Enter into real heart faith and cast the care over on Him.

Which things are an allegory: for these are the two covenants; the one from the mount Sinai, which gendereth to bondage, which is Hagar.

For this Hagar is Mount Sinai in Arabia, and answereth to Jerusalem which now is, and is in bondage with her children.

But Jerusalem which is above is free, which is the mother of us all.

For it is written, rejoice, thou barren that bearest not . . . .

Galatians 4:24-27a

Who is Paul referring to in this last verse? He is speaking of the spirit rejoicing that it cannot bear. Why? Because God does not want you to bear on your own. That is why He cuts away the flesh so that you don't bear something, create or initiate something, through it. We cannot create our own healing or salvation, but we try. Even spiritual principles will not work until the soul man is in the proper perspective, and the principles are channeled through the spirit.

. . . Break forth and cry, thou that travailest not: for the desolate hath many more children than she which hath an husband.

Galatians 4:27

God says that He will bring forth more through those who are not married than through those that are married and have a husband. He is saying, "I will do more through your spirit that cannot bring forth without My touch than through your soul and flesh which can create all kinds of things." We see that the value is in the spirit, but this is where the soul rebels. The soul man does not like the ways of God. He does not like to wait on God. The soul man must be taught to wait and not initiate.

> **Now we, brethren, as Isaac was, are the children of promise.**
>
> **But as then he that was born after the flesh persecuted him that was born after the spirit, even so it is now.**
>
> Galatians 4:28,29

The natural man does not understand the things of God. The unregenerate man persecuted the regenerate one. When you get born again, you war against yourself. But here is the beauty of the *merismos:*

> **Nevertheless what saith the scripture? Cast out the bondwoman and her son; for the son of the bondwoman shall not be heir with the son of the free woman.**
>
> Galatians 4:30

The only way to be sure that you will be heir of it all is to get rid of the other guy who wants to be heir of it all. You are going to have to deal with Hagar, who keeps producing babies. Don't just pluck the fruit, sever the root. Don't just get rid of the "Ishmaels," cast out the bondwoman, also. Why? Because "Hagars" (the soul) are reproducers of Ishmaels. Quit conceiving

Ishmaels through reasonings and intellect. Learn the ways of God.

And so it is written, The first man Adam was made a living soul; the last Adam was made a quickening spirit.

Howbeit that was not first which is spiritual, but that which is natural; and afterward that which is spiritual.

The first man is of the earth, earthy: the second man is the Lord from heaven.

As is the earthy, such are they also that are earthy: and as is the heavenly, such are they also that are heavenly.

And as we have borne the image of the earthly, we shall also bear the image of the heavenly.

I Corinthians 15:45-49

The first thing man wants to do is natural. The first thought is from the soulish realm. Man's first choice is self-motivated because the soul is self-ruled. He goes to the Tree of the Knowledge of Good and Evil. The soul goes the way of all the earth. He thinks like mere man. Man has helped God fulfill a lot of promises, but God is not pleased with those Ishmaels. If you conceive it, God will let you raise it, and it will cost you plenty. Ishmaels are expensive. Some of you have bought cars that were Ishmaels and homes that were Ishmaels. God has promised us cars and homes, but let *Him* perform it. God has promised us Isaacs, not Ishmaels.

In 1 Peter 5:2, the apostle told the elders to "take the oversight." In Hebrews 13:17, the writer said, **Obey them that have the rule over you, and submit**

yourselves: for they watch for your souls. The very purpose of bishops and overseers is to oversee, or "see over," the soul. People who are constantly coming up with the idea that they don't want to be joined to a local church usually are not wanting the bishop ministry to bring oversight to their souls. "Well! I don't have to go to that church!" There goes Hagar again — rebellious and independent rather than submissive.

If you are going to be a doer of the Word, you have to do all of it. You need to begin to confess:

> *"Father, in the name of Jesus, I thank you that I am in obedience to Your Word. I believe it. The Word is true in my life. I submit to it, for it is the final authority over me. The elders watch over my soul, and I receive with joy this ministry of oversight. My soul moves into submission to Your Word."*

So then, Brethren, we are not children of the bondwoman, but of the free (Gal. 4:23). I am not a child of *psuche.* I am not a child of Hagar. I am not an Ishmael. I am a son of promise, and my spirit man is free to receive from God what He has promised me *of a surety.* God sent Jesus to seal that covenant and to say that I have a surety of a better covenant. Jesus came as the absolute of the covenant. Whatever God told Abraham, being his seed, God shows me as He did Abraham, the surety of how to receive.

Although I didn't want it at first, I am so glad that He walked between my spirit and soul by His Word. I am so glad that I did not run from the "operation." I am so glad that I submitted myself so that I could be dealt with and come out as someone who would glorify Christ and release the Spirit of God to people rather than my personality or popularity or all the other garbage that goes along with that kind of soul-thinking.

I am glad to be able to bring forth Christ and Him crucified, knowing that **I am crucified with Christ: nevertheless I live, yet not I, but Christ liveth in me** (Gal. 2:20). In Christ I really do live and move and have my being. (Acts 17:28.) I have been made conformable to His death. (Phil. 3:10.)

Everyone wants to know Him and the power of His resurrection, but we also must know the fellowship. of His sufferings, being made conformable to His death. His death in that verse was the laying down of His life — His *psuche*. I want to be conformed to the death of *psuche*. I want to know what it means to lose my life so that I may live and breathe His life and release the power of His beauty, but we resist words in the Body of Christ such as "His sufferings" or "brokenness."

If you do not break the outer, you will never come forth with the beauty of the inner. People say, "God won't break your will, brother." Oh, yes, He will! But only after you "will" to fall upon the Rock. (Matt. 21:44.) He won't while you are in rebellion, but He will cause brokenness to come if you fall upon the Rock and say, "God forgive me for my soulish activities." When you do that, He so graciously breaks that will.

He is the potter, and you are the clay. He is constantly using His two-edged sword to cut out of you all of those things that are keeping you from walking and experiencing His best. His purpose is not to hurt you but to get you into a position to experience the resurrection power and blessings of the covenant.

This breaking will not take your identity from you. It will not squelch your personality. It will cause you to be livelier and more vibrant than you have ever been before, because it will allow the personality to come forth under the governorship of your spirit.

How do I do this? I keep my spirit and soul segregated in my mind constantly. Even though my soul has been dealt with and reunited with my spirit under submission, I do not give him any opportunity. At any given time, he may seek his own way; however, I remind my soul that if he will decrease, he will increase. If he seeks to save himself, he will lose. Faith is of the spirit, but hope is an anchor for the soul. I don't rob my soul man of his hope, but the hope he has is an expectation from the Lord.

When conflict comes, I go and lay prostrate before God. I say, "God, there is a war going on in me. I want your life, and I want my life. Now when I come out of this, I am going to find out if my spirit man is stronger than my soul, because two are going in the ring, and one is going to get whipped. I am trusting you, God. I believe the Greater One is in my spirit, and He will win."

If you do this, however, every reason and logical excuse for not going God's way will come into your mind during that time of battle. There is only *one* reason why you need to go God's way: **To obey is better than sacrifice** (1 Sam. 15:12). When your soul acts up, begin taking the Word of God and counter him with the final authority, God's Word, so that your house will not remain divided against itself.

PART II
THE REALM OF THE SOUL

4
"PSUCHE SOUFFLE"

We have found the enemy — it is us. We have found that our souls are the seat, or the source, of most of the problems we have in conforming to the image of Jesus. We need to know ourselves, and that means submitting to the two-edged sword's division of us into separate parts. The first *merismos* of the soul is to divide the soulish realm into three areas: mind, will, and emotions. But that is not all of the possible separation. "Dividing asunder" in Hebrews 4:12 means to take the myriad facets of your life, break them down, and clarify them. Each of the three main divisions of the soul can be divided into five categories.

Areas of the Soul

The *mind* can be divided into the areas of imagination, reasoning, thought, logic, and intellect — all summed up in one word: understanding. In dealing with the soul, one of the primary things that will be encountered is the desire to possess knowledge. Through the above five functions, the soul man will accumulate information for the purpose of coming to a conclusion.

There is, however, a higher way. It is called "revelation knowledge." This is knowledge revealed to the spirit of man. The spirit man goes to the Tree of Life, while the soul man goes to the Tree of Knowledge of Good and Evil. The soul wants knowledge, but he must be directed to partake of the right tree and get knowledge the right way — by revelation of the Word, not by accumulation of information. The light or understanding of a man is the life. **In him was life** (zoe); **and the life was the light of men** (John 1:4).

The next area of the soul is the *will*. The will is made up of decision, choice, intent, purpose, and desire. These five areas are summed up in *determination*.

The third and final major area of the soul is the *emotions*. Emotions are made up of the five physical senses: sight, taste, touch, smell, and hearing. Also within this realm are other things such as hatred, love, and so forth.

In studying these three main areas of the soul — mind, will, and emotions — we find the categories that describe the soulish activity in our lives. This will reveal to us the things that make us do what we do and will show us why, although we are born again and Spirit filled, we continue to act as if we are not. We will understand better by looking at Genesis 2:7.

And the Lord God formed man of the dust of the ground, and breathed into his nostrils the breath of life; and man became a living soul.

Genesis 2:7

In the Hebrew, the word for soul is *nephesh;* and, in the Greek, the word is *psuche.* Both words mean "a living soul." Translated another way, the words can mean "an independent lifestyle." Can the soul man live independent of God? Of course it can. You lived independent of God until the time you invited Him into your life. You made the choice to live your own life until your new birth.

What really happened that caused the soul man to have such independence? When God made man a living soul, the living soul became the life of the personality, or a unique individual. The soul is called the seat of the personality. You are an individual. God did not make clones. He created man with the potential to have individual personalities, but He never intended man to be independent of Him.

However, in most areas of ministry, many get cloned very quickly, and that is not what God wants. The copying of successful ministries happens because the personality or soul man of the aspiring minister is trying to achieve what should only be achieved by the spirit man through the Holy Spirit. We receive knowledge from the Word of God, but the only thing that should be conforming our personalities is the character of Jesus.

I don't allow any other teaching or ministry to affect and change my individuality. When that happens, the thing you are following becomes a god to your soul. Perhaps it's a low form of a god, not highly developed, but it is still a form of idolatry. You must watch your soul. He will bow to something, and when he is drawn to it, he will become like it. When you begin to take on the traits and characteristics of someone else, then you have a problem. Unless your soul man knows how to draw upon God and extract the Spirit and Word from whatever is being taught, he tends to conform to the image of the admired leader. Don't become like whoever is teaching. Become like the Word of God which they are teaching.

Where did man become a living personality? Perhaps a better way to put it would be "living through personality" or "living his personality." When God breathed into man the breath of life, he became (or came to a place) where he could express or live his personality. He could demonstrate it, and God was not offended by it. God is not offended by your uniqueness, individuality, or personality — although some people may be!

> **And out of the ground made the Lord God to grow every tree that is pleasant to the sight, and good for food; the tree of life also in the midst of the garden, and the tree of knowledge of good and evil.**

> **Genesis 2:9**

Notice the term **knowledge of good and evil.** Within it lies the problem.

The Beginning of Self-Consciousness

In Genesis 2, we find God giving the man the opportunity to choose. Where does the power of choice come from? The soul man actually carries out the act of choosing, but, in God's original design, the spirit man was to govern or dictate the choices of the soul.

> **And the Lord God took the man, and put him into the garden of Eden *to dress it and to keep it.***

> **Genesis 2:15**

Here is the oversight of the soul. You are God's garden, and your spirit is called to be a husbandman over that garden.

> **And the Lord God commanded the man, saying, Of every tree of the garden thou mayest freely eat:**

But of the tree of the knowledge of good and evil, thou shalt not eat of it: for in the day that thou eatest thereof thou shalt surely die (or, in dying thou shalt die).

Genesis 2:16,17

God had commanded Adam and Eve not to partake of the Tree of *the* Knowledge of Good and Evil. In their disobedience, something very strange and different happened to them. Let's read Genesis 3.

Now the serpent was more subtle than any beast of the field which the Lord God had made. And he said unto the woman, Yea, hath God said, Ye shall not eat of every tree of the garden?

And the woman said unto the serpent, We may eat of the fruit of the trees of the garden:

But of the fruit of the tree which is in the midst of the garden, God hath said, Ye shall not eat of it, neither shall ye touch it, lest ye die.

And the serpent said unto the woman, Ye shall not surely die.

For God doth know that in the day ye eat thereof, then your eyes shall be opened, and ye shall be as gods, knowing good and evil.

And when the woman saw that the tree was good for food, and that it was pleasant to the eyes, and a tree to be desired to make one wise, she took of the fruit thereof, and did eat, and gave also unto her husband with her; and he did eat.

And the eyes of them both were opened, and they knew that they were naked; and they sewed fig leaves together, and made themselves aprons.

And they heard the voice of the Lord God walking in the garden in the cool of the day; and Adam and his wife hid themselves from the presence of the Lord God amongst the trees of the garden.

And the Lord God called unto Adam, and said unto him, Where art thou?

And he said, I heard thy voice in the garden, and I was afraid, because I was naked; and I hid myself.

And he said, Who told thee that thou wast naked? Hast thou eaten of the tree, whereof I commanded thee that thou shouldest not eat?

Genesis 3:1-11

Notice, in verse 7, as soon as they ate of the forbidden fruit, they became aware of themselves and realized that they were naked and opened. This is the beginning of self-awareness and self-realization, as well as self-consciousness, which caused them to try to hide shame, guilt, and sin with fig-leaf aprons. They were naked and opened. Their lives were obvious and exposed. This also was the beginning of self-preservation. What followed was a conversation full of self-defense, self-justification, and other excuses for self.

Adam and Eve's disobedience brought upon humanity the whole soulish world. I have coined a phrase which, to me, sums up the characteristics of the soulish realm: "*psuche* souffle." The soul man became a recipe for selfishness, a world of selfishness personified. The ingredients are self-indulgence, self-preservation, self-defense, self-motivation, self-centeredness, self-appreciation, self-love, self-adoration, self-worship. The soul is self, and self is the soul. The soul *is* man's personality. It is himself.

Man has, through the years, exploited the world of self and produced books and teachings on self-esteem, self-worth, self-image, self-value. The soul uses anything it can to *hide* the shame and guilt that lies in it. The self-ruled man needs salvation in Christ, not salvation through self-improvement programs.

The soul always goes to *the* Tree of Knowledge of Good and Evil because it appeals to the intellect and to the senses. The soul is full of pride and arrogance. He is commanding, domineering, rude, crude, ill-mannered, and inconsiderate. He is loud, boastful, talkative, and opinionated. He is showy, demonstrative, flashy, and obnoxious. He is full of insecurities, fears, intimidations, and inhibitions. He is introverted and extroverted. He is critical, judgmental, condescending, and condemning. He is self-sufficient, self-reliant, self-motivating, and self-seeking. He is self-love and self-adoration. He is *idolatry*, which is self-worship. *He is selfish*. Look at Genesis 1:26-28.

> **And God said, Let us make man in our image, after our likeness: and let them have dominion over the fish of the sea, and over the fowl of the air, and over the cattle, and over all the earth, and over every creeping thing that creepeth upon the earth.**
>
> **So God created man in his own image, in the image of God created he him; male and female created he them.**
>
> **And God blessed them, and God said unto them, Be fruitful, and multiply, and**

51

replenish the earth, and subdue it: and have dominion over the fish of the sea, and over the fowl of the air, and over every living thing that moveth upon the earth.

If God made man after His image and likeness, what part of man was to have authority? The spirit of man is to have authority, because only in the spirit is there authority for dominion. What did God give man authority over? He gave him authority over everything that is dualistic, or body and soul. There is no authority in the soulish realm. There is intimidation, exploitation, and manipulation, but no authority. All authority is given to Jesus, and He does not use it in the soulish realm. His disciples, as well as His enemies, tried to get him to, but he refused. He did not demonstrate His power through the soul to prove anything to anybody, but He did minister His authority through His spirit to do the work of God.

The Spirit Man Has Oversight

You are spirit, soul, and body. Your spirit is to have oversight and preeminence over your soul. Why? Because when God told man to take dominion over all the earth, the only thing made in His image and likeness was mankind. Man is the only thing on earth that is triune. Only man possesses a spirit. All other things are dualistic, body and soul. The soul is to be dominated, not by breaking it, but by training it. To break a horse is the impatience of ego. To train a horse is the patience of the soul. **In your patience possess ye your souls** (Luke 21:19).

Hupomone is the Greek word for "patience." It means "consistency." Through consistency, you will bring control to the soul. Even children, who are triune in nature, are dualistic in function until they are born again. Until then, they operate dualistically. Therefore, God has placed them under the authority of the parents — not under the parents' souls but under their spirits.

When your child begins to push and demands to get, deny that behavior. You should not permit such behavior in them any more than your heavenly Father permits it in you. It just doesn't work.

When Adam became a living soul, or lived his individuality or uniqueness through the soulish realm, he had the spirit man as governor over his soul. A horse has no spirit, therefore it has no controlling factor except the soul. The souls of horses, as all of creation, have been affected by the fall, and they want to go their own ways. If you leave them without oversight, they will be worthless. They are wild and uncontrollable. You can't control them or tend to them.

When Satan came to Adam and Eve in the garden, he appealed to their abilities to choose. He wanted them to make a choice. What should Adam have done if he had rebuked the devil? He should have taken dominion over his own soul, brought oversight to it and, in so doing, brought it into submission to the spirit by saying, "Wait a minute, soul. You have no right to move independently unless you confer with me. I am the one who governs by life or death the decisions you are about to make. I am your umpire. I will settle with finality every question that arises in you. I will let you know whether it is the Tree of Life or the Tree of Knowledge of Good and Evil." This is the way of God. To this day, you are not to go to the Tree of Knowledge of Good and Evil. You must partake of that which is life and peace. You will not know what is life and peace in your soulish realm until you learn to confer with your spirit, and until your spirit emanates the *zoe*, or the life of God, on decisions. It may be good for me to go preach, but if it is not God's direction, then it still produces death. If there is no *zoe*, there is no "go-ey" for me!

When you were born again, you lost the right to be your own God. You are no longer your judge. When you think you are, then self or soul becomes the deciding factor between what is right and wrong for you. You will judge where you will go, what you will do, where you will live, and where you will work. All of that is out of order. Your soul does not have that privilege, power, or authority. The only reason the soul usurps authority is because the spirit does not take the preeminence. The spirit wants what is of God, while the soul wants what is of self. That is why Christians who go to college to find their vocations fail so often. It is out of order. Only God has the privilege to tell you what He has called you to be. After you find your call in Christ, then you can go where He tells you to go in order to prepare. *Jesus is God, not you!*

"Naked and Opened"

In Genesis 3:7, Adam and Eve became aware of themselves. They had been naked and opened before God prior to their sin, but it was not until afterwards that they became aware of self. The moment they sinned, they were introduced to "self-awareness."

> **Neither is there any creature that is not manifest in his sight: but all things are *naked and opened* unto the eyes of him with whom we have to do.**
>
> **Hebrews 4:13**

There are three stages to awareness in life: spirit; which is God-consciousness; soul, which is self-consciousness; and body, which is material, or world-consciousness. These three levels are those with which we deal in life. We come into self-consciousness shortly after being born. In a matter of a few months, a baby begins to develop its own likes and dislikes and wants. Self really begins to possess you if you suddenly catch a glimpse of yourself in a store window and stop to examine your reflection. You become very aware of yourself. If you are not careful, you will end up with a con job from the devil. If he can't convince you that you are terrific, then he will convince you that you are ugly. Either way, you are aware of self.

When Adam and Eve became aware of themselves, that was the beginning of the *psuche* realm. Once they became self-aware, their first actions were to cover up themselves. They moved into the world of self-preservation, self-defense, self-justification, and all the other things with which man covers himself. All of them are fig leaves and aprons. *But we are still naked and opened before God regardless of what we use as a cover.* Yet we continue to try to preserve ourselves with excuses and reasons. We try to justify our actions and words. Before we can be dealt with, we must remove all those "fig leaves and aprons."

Notice that Jesus said, "If you seek to save your life (*psuche*), you will lose it." (Luke 17:33.) The moment you sought to preserve it, you just lost it. The day you choose it, you lose it. You fight to excuse the soul life, but your excuses are so obvious to those around you who are spiritual. When you find out from the Word of God about the soul man, you will stop coming to his defense and let him get dealt with and corrected.

You need to be aligned properly. Your spirit is the real man. Your soul is the part that is going to get you in trouble. Stop speaking up for him and preserving him and backing him up with support and, for once, turn on him and watch what he does. However, we don't want to do that because, after all, we are so wonderful!

By not allowing our spirits to have preeminence, we live the self lifestyle, and it has kept us in bondage. All of the self things keep us from realizing the Christ life within us. You need to say to your soul:

"Because I have met Jesus, my spirit man is alive. Soul, you have been on the throne, but I am dethroning you now. You have done what you wanted to do, thought what you wanted to think, and imagined all kinds of imaginations. You have justified yourself and made excuses for your life. Now, you have just come to an end. Another, called the *pneumatikos* man, is on the throne. He is a spiritual man, and he is going to rule your life. You are in trouble from this day onward. I will no longer preserve you or defend you. I am going to strip from you all the aprons and fig leaves and make you stand before God naked and opened, completely exposed and manifested."

Any time that I begin to see soulish inclinations in myself, I get right on it. Take that *psuche* man and *merismos* him. See yourself as spirit and soul, and put the soul where he belongs. Put a whip in the hand of the spirit man and let him bring discipline to the soul. If you will, God will cause your soul to be dealt with through your spirit, and you will be brought into proper alignment and grow up in Christ in all things.

Where people have constantly misunderstood the conflict within man, not knowing the *merismos* teaching, is in trying to live a "crucified life." God does not want your personality dead. He wants us to *reckon* ourselves dead, meaning "no longer independent." He wants us to be subservient to the spirit man and no longer moving independently of God. My spirit has the authority in the earth over my soul.

People who are always going around trying to "kill" themselves are misunderstanding the problem. Why? Because those who are trying to live the crucified life never get to enjoy the resurrected lifestyle, which is the realm of spirit raised above soul. That is the realm in which I am going to live.

Divine Authority

There is authority returning to the earth, and it is called "divine authority." In time to come, wherever you go, someone's spirit will have oversight of your soul. This is Aaron's rod. It is blossoming, for it has returned through the Ark of the Covenant (God's Word), and wherever you go, you will experience divine authority. We might as well get used to it. Submit to God's way and rejoice, thanking God for it.

The main reason many people will not get involved in a local body is because they do not want anyone over them. I have heard people say that specifically: "I don't want anyone over me." Sure enough, no one is over them, not even Jesus. Because of the extremes which occurred in the "shepherding movement," many people say, "Jesus is my covering." Many Christians will not allow anyone to provide oversight to them. Jesus, the Chief Shepherd, wants to place us in local sheepfolds (churches) to bring oversight through undershepherds.

This is the purpose of the "bishop ministry" that God established as shown in the New Testament. However, those who have oversight are to be over us from their spirits, not from their souls.

The problem has been that many in authority were operating through the soulish realm. When someone lets a position of oversight "go to his head" and begins to try to force people to submit, it hinders God and hurts the church and the people involved. Dominion by the soul is only offensive and undermining. We must realize that there *is* divine authority that is of God and comes from the spirit. Even in the local church, there is a distinct personality, a uniqueness.

For ye were as sheep going astray; but are now returned unto the shepherd and bishop of your souls.

1 Peter 2:25

Here is the two-fold work of the pastor: shepherd and bishop of the soul.

The Israelites became fearful while Moses was on the mountain. They said, "Moses, you speak to us, not God, lest we die." (Ex. 20:19.) That is what people want, because if it is just Moses, we can argue with him, but how can we argue with God? We can't. We either submit to God or resist Him, and God resists the resistor.

And so it is written, The first man Adam was made a living soul (psuche); the last Adam was made a quickening spirit.

Howbeit that was not first which is spiritual (pneumatikos), but that which is natural (psuchikos); and afterward that which is spiritual.

1 Corinthians 15:45,46

This is a type of our own lives. When you were born from your mother's womb, you became a living soul, an individual with personality. When you are born of flesh, you are flesh. And Jesus said, . . . **the flesh profiteth nothing** (John 6:63). The principle in these verses is this: That which is first is soulish, soul-controlled and ruled. Then, afterward, comes that which is spirit, or ruled by the spirit.

The first man is of the earth, earthy: the second man is the Lord from heaven.

As is the earthy, such are they also that are earthy: and as is the heavenly, such are they also that are heavenly.

1 Corinthians 15:47,48

In other words, you are going to express the image of the earth or of heaven. You will manifest the characteristics of one or the other. The apostle Paul is telling us here that the soul man, which is born of the flesh, is first. There is the problem. The first thing is usually *your* idea. The first tree is the wrong tree. The first choice you make is the wrong choice, until you get the soul man into a position where he is no longer first.

Remember when Jesus spoke to those he called to follow him? (Luke 9:57-62.) They all said, "Let me first . . . and then I will." Jesus said none of them were worthy of the kingdom. "I'll be glad to, as soon as I . . . ." God does not mind you having other pursuits, but the first thing should be His things: spirit, soul, and body. **But seek ye first the kingdom of God, and his righteousness; and all these things shall be added unto you** (Matt. 6:33).

If you will pick up on this principle, it will change your lifestyle. The first thing many Christians do when they go into a new place is look for a job. At that moment, they are being led by livelihood and vocation. Second, they look for a school for their children. Last of all, they look for a church to attend. Instead of that which is spiritual leading, they follow what is natural. That is out of order. The first thing should be to go where God is happening, to a church that has the flow and the go of the move of God. After that, God will give you the right job and the right school.

You may say, "But Brother Randy, I can't go there. They don't have the kind of job I need." Then we know what controls you and what is your god. "But if I leave, I'll lose my prestige and position." This sounds like pride and is of the soulish realm: self-value, self-worth, and self-importance. It is all *psuche*. No, you have to do what Peter, James, and John did. When Jesus called them, they dropped what they were doing and followed Him. When God gives something to you, you can enjoy it. Rather than being ruled by it, serving it, or living for it, it serves you.

The realm of *psuche* is the realm of idolatry and the worship of self. It begins out of self-awareness, self-adoration, then goes into self-love which takes you into self-worship, which is idolizing yourself. When you do that, you will create gods to serve you. We were created to serve God, then He will meet our needs, but because people are caught up in this little world of self-awareness, it is pathetic what happens — *psuche* souffle.

The order of first things is: you must put a watchman over your soul until he has been dealt with. Then you keep the watchman there to maintain order so that the soul does not get out of line again. Your soul is no different from anyone else's. If you do not keep oversight, your soul man will go *his* way, which is a way that seems right to you. It is a broad way. That is what the soul wants — plenty of room. However, the way of the spirit is a narrow way. It takes a lot of wisdom, oversight, and dealings with your soul, to walk it.

Those who walk in the spirit and are led of the spirit are the sons, *huios* (fully matured sons), of God. They have grown up to maturity, and the Father can give them responsibilities. Jesus knew that the Father had **given all things into his hands** (John 13:3). If you truly want to become a mature son of God, pray the following prayer of commitment.

Prayer

Father, I come before You right now, and I want to thank you in the name of Jesus Christ that I repent of those selfish, egotistical, arrogant, prideful, boastful, domineering, commanding, and pushy attitudes — those areas where I think I am so good. Although I have been made good in the spirit, You are dealing with my soul. I determine to put off the things of my own lifestyle and to put on the preciousness of Christ, even in my soul.

I am asking you to forgive me where I have "psuched" out, where I have chosen my own life and lived naturally by my first choice, doing what I wanted to do.

I now confess that I am no longer my own. I was bought with a price. I confess Jesus as my Lord. Now, I believe that He is just that. I do not have the right to live my life, to do what I want to do, or to go where I want to go.

From this time on, I renounce the Tree of Knowledge of Good and Evil. I am a partaker of the Tree of Life. Jesus, You are life unto me. Your Word is spirit and life. It is final authority over me. I go to it. I confide in it. I believe it. I accept it. I walk in it. I obey it. Your Word is final authority in my life. I will do what You say to do, go where You tell me to go, because I am bought with a price. I really am not my own. I am crucified with Christ, nevertheless I live, yet not "psuche," but Christ in me, the life of the spirit.

I will be led by Your Spirit, controlled by Your Spirit, possessed by the Spirit of God. Spirit, soul, and body, from this time on, I begin to align myself by the order of first things.

I follow and pursue hard after the apostolic order of my life. My spirit has the preeminence, my soul is subservient, and my body is just a carrier of the things of God. In Jesus name. Amen.

5
SAVING OF THE SOUL

We have already dealt with the first phase of the *merismos* teaching: revelation for illumination. We are now going to look into phase two: separation for clarification, and how God begins to deal with us. When the Word of God comes, it always brings with it revelation. Next, the Word moves you into a position for transfiguration, a position where your life is changed and altered to conform with the Word. Once you have changed and altered your lifestyle, you are brought into the manifestation of that Word, a place where the Word becomes flesh, or a way of life.

Each of these stages are progressive steps encountered in the Christian life. However, you must understand that *just because you go through these stages does not mean that you will receive them.* **He made known his ways unto Moses, his acts unto the children of Israel** (Ps. 103:7). We are to be thankful for all of the gifts, signs, wonders, and manifestations of the Holy Spirit in our lives, but they have nothing to do with our character or with understanding the ways of God. We must learn the way He is and the way He operates. God never changes. Once we find the way of God, absolutes can rise up within us.

In this chapter, I will be dealing with the saving of the soul. The soul needs to be saved, and the Word says, . . . **he that winneth souls is wise** (Prov. 11:30). Let me deal for a moment with your religious mentality. I am really one of the true soul winners. By the Word of God, I am to save souls. You do not have to be wise to win spirits. I do not mean that in a derogatory way, but really, it does not take a lot of wisdom to lead someone into the new birth. All you need is obedience and John 3:16 and Romans 10:9,10 to be packed with ammunition. However, you have to move in the mind of Christ and extract the wisdom of God to learn how to save a soul. *Souls are not saved in the same manner as spirits.*

Let's take a look at the ways in which God deals. The word *save* in the Greek is *sozo*. It means to be made whole or complete. Sometimes, it is translated as healing, deliverance, or wholeness. It is an all-inclusive word. Salvation for the spirit comes instantly; salvation for the soul comes progressively; salvation for the body comes in the future. That is why you have to use faith to keep the law of sin and death from bringing sickness to your body.

And the very God of peace sanctify you wholly; and I pray God your whole spirit and soul and body be preserved blameless unto the coming of our Lord Jesus Christ.

1 Thessalonians 5:23

Paul was talking here about "wholly," complete in totality. God wants to do a total work of sanctifying you. *To sanctify* means "to separate, set apart, or set aside." God wants to bring separation. Jesus is the Word, and He separates. In Luke 12:51, He said, **Suppose ye that I am come to give peace on earth? I tell you, Nay; but rather division** (*diamerismos* — disunion, a channel of separation or division). There is a *whole* spirit, *whole* soul, and *whole* body, yet each whole is the product of the parts. Therefore, the parts can be *merismosed*.

Notice **be preserved** in 1 Thessalonians 5:23. You can take fruit, such as strawberries, and make what is called preserves, but *before* you preserve them, you wash them thoroughly in water to cleanse them from any impurities. That is exactly what God wants to do with your soul. **That he might sanctify and cleanse it with the washing of water by the word** (Eph. 5:26). There will be no preserving *until* the soul has been dealt with by the water.

There may be some areas of your *psuche* that are being washed. Some areas may be sanctified, while others may be preserved, but there are still areas that need a real work of God. The plan of God is to preserve your *whole* soul. **Faithful is he that calleth you, who also will do it** (1 Thess. 5:24).

The Engrafted Word

Let us look at some other scriptures. We are dealing with the saving (*sozo*) of the soul.

> **Wherefore lay apart all filthiness and superfluity of naughtiness, and receive with meekness the *engrafted word*, which is able to *save your souls*.**
>
> **James 1:21**

We are talking about the whole soul — mind, will, and emotions — being sanctified and preserved. It is not just the Word, but the *engrafted Word* that has the power to save your soul. Owning a Bible and reading it now and then will not save your soul. The word *engrafted (emphutos)* is the revelation for the saving of the soul. The Word must become embedded in your *psuche*. The Greek word is derived from two other words. *En* means "a fixed position" and *phuo* means

65

"to puff or to blow up," or "to germinate," or "to grow." The Word of God is to continue growing from a blade to an ear to a full corn. It will not grow up in you, however, unless you have it planted in a fixed position. As you plant the Word, embed it into your soul in a fixed position. The Word will save your soul, depending on how much of the Word you will receive.

The term *with meekness* gives you an attitude with which to align yourself. You must approach the Word of God in submission to it. Usually the soul man rejects it in anger, hostility, pride, and arrogance and retains its own opinions. That is all "*psuche* souffle." What you must learn to do is get your spirit man over your soul and, when the Word of God comes forth, correct your soul attitude and receive the Word with meekness.

> Now the just shall live by faith: but if any man draw back, my soul shall have no pleasure in him.

> But we are not of them who draw back unto perdition; but of them that believe to the saving of the soul.

Hebrews 10:38,39

The writer does not just say "believe in the saving of the soul" but believe *to* the saving of the soul. The way to handle the gospel is to believe in it before you believe *for* it. That is where a lot of people have gotten into trouble. They did not really believe in the Word, so when they tried to believe for it to work, it didn't. The engrafted, implanted Word was not in them.

Remember that the Word of God is the only thing that will separate the spirit and soul. *The engrafted Word* is also the only thing that will save the soul. You must take the Word of God and embed it into your thoughts.

As you allow it to remain fixed there, it will bring salvation to your soul. *You* cannot save yourself. People too often try to change themselves when they see something they don't like, but they cannot do that. We are not talking about psychology or psychiatry or turning introspective and trying to change through will power. Change can only be done by the Word of God. The Word deals with my soul and saves me.

For we are *his* workmanship, created in Christ Jesus unto good works . . . .

Ephesians 2:10

For it is *God* which worketh in you both to will and to do of his good pleasure.

Philippians 2:13

Once God works it in, then you need to do what Philippians 2:12 says, **. . . work out your own salvation with fear and trembling.** In other words, demonstrate God's inward work by an outward showing forth. Does God want to work in your soul and save it? Yes!

Being confident of this very thing, that he which hath begun a good work *in* you will perform it (finish it) **until the day of Jesus Christ.**

Philippians 1:6

Beloved, I wish above all things that thou mayest prosper and be in health, even as thy soul prospereth.

3 John 2

Problems have stemmed from the fact that people would not leave the Word in them long enough to let it save them. The degree to which I am prospering in my soul will be the degree to which I will prosper and be in health, to the same identical measure. That is why it is necessary to **receive the** *engrafted* **Word,** the only thing that will save your soul. We have had a lot of views, opinions, beliefs, and ideas that have kept us from prospering and being in health. We must have our souls saved. Let the Word do its work.

Let me repeat it one more time: *Everyone who has been saved in his spirit needs to be saved in his soul.* The salvation of the spirit was instantaneous, but the work of the engrafted Word is progressive.

The Heart of Man

By the study of the Word, I have seen that spirit and heart are not the same thing. The Greek word for *spirit* is *pneuma.* The Greek word for *heart* is *kardia.* The two Hebrew words used in the Old Testament are also different. I have not tied them together as one, so I have been able to see what they really mean.

The heart truly is the center, the core of a man, but what are the components of the heart? They are the spirit *and* the soul. Let's see why. We know that when we are born again, we receive an instantaneous birth in the spirit man, but can you doubt in your heart? Mark 11:23 says that you can. Are you doubting in your spirit? Matthew 12:34b,35 and James 3:10,11 say:

For out of the abundance of the heart the mouth speaketh.

A good man out of the good treasure of the heart bringeth forth good things: and an evil man out of the evil treasure bringeth forth evil things.

Out of the *same* **mouth proceedeth blessing and cursing . . . sweet water and bitter.**

Do these things really come out of the hearts of born again people? Of course, but *not* out of their spirits. It is impossible for evil to come out of a spirit that has been born of incorruptible seed that liveth and abideth forever. No, the cursing and bitter water do not come out of my spirit but out of the soul part of my heart. We can even do the will of God from our souls:

Not with eyeservice, as menpleasers; but as the servants of Christ, doing the will of God from the heart (psuche).

Ephesians 6:6

Where do we receive the will of God? We receive it in the spirit. From where do we perform the will of God? We perform it in the heart which, in the verse above, is the Greek word for soul. So, if you are going to be a doer of the Word, the soul man is going to have to cooperate, and the only way he will cooperate is to get him saved with the engrafted Word.

When God brings correction and chastisement, it is to the soul of man. The spirit is in harmony and submission to God. The problem is in the soul, and that is the part of man that God corrects.

And ye have forgotten the exhortation which speaketh unto you as unto children, My son, despise not thou the chastening of the Lord, nor faint when thou art rebuked of him.

If ye endure chastening, God dealeth with you as with sons; for what son is he whom the father chasteneth not?

Hebrews 12:5,7

The three words, *despise, faint, and endure,* all deal with the soul area. Notice Hebrews 12:3: **For consider him that endured such contradiction of sinners against** himself, lest ye be wearied and faint in your minds (*psuche*). It is in the soul of man that one grows weary, faints, despises, or endures.

The Divided Heart

What is idolatry? Idolatry is self-love, because the idols you build are for the purpose of serving you.

Then will I sprinkle clean water upon you, and ye shall be clean: from all your filthiness, and from all your idols, will I cleanse you.

A new heart also will I give you, and a new spirit will I put within you: and I will take away the stony heart out of your flesh, and I will give you an heart of flesh.

And I will put my spirit within you, and cause you to walk in my statutes, and ye shall keep my judgments, and do them.

Ezekiel 36:25-27

And I will give them one heart, and I will put a new spirit within you; and I will take the stony heart out of their flesh, and will give them an heart of flesh:

That they may walk in my statutes, and keep mine ordinances, and do them: and they shall be my people, and I will be their God.

Ezekiel 11:19,20

Notice what kind of heart God will give you, a *new* heart and *one* heart. At the moment of your new birth, you were divided. You became a house divided against itself: your love for Jesus versus your love for self, desires, and aspirations for things above *and* for things below. What happens if the house remains divided

70

against itself? It will fall. The whole purpose of this teaching is to keep you from falling, to help you get your soul dealt with by God and brought back into union with your spirit, making you of one heart.

God wants to take out of you the stony heart, the rebellion, disobedience, and hardness. Yes, He does, but remember in what area — the soul. He does not want you to have inward conflict and struggle and jockeying for position and control between the spirit and the soul. He wants you to be flexible, pliable, sensitive, submissive, and obedient.

> **Jesus saith unto them, Did ye never read in the scriptures, The stone which the builders rejected, the same is become the head of the corner: this is the Lord's doing, and it is marvellous in our eyes?**
>
> **Therefore say I unto you, The kingdom of God shall be taken from you, and given to a nation bringing forth the fruits thereof.**
>
> **And whosoever shall fall on this stone shall be broken: but on whomsoever it shall fall, it will grind him to powder.**
>
> **Matthew 21:42-44**

God's Word said that He would take out of us a stony heart. Is Jesus Christ the rock? When your heart of stone falls upon the rock of Christ, you will be broken, but if you keep resisting Him, you will be turned to powder. It is much easier to willingly lay upon Him and ask forgiveness for being wrong. When God brings correction by His Word, don't despise it. **Receive with meekness the engrafted word, which is able to save your souls** (James 1:21). If you resist His Word, He is equally clear on what He will do:

71

Likewise, ye younger, submit yourselves unto the elder. Yea, all of you be subject one to another, and be clothed with humility: for God resisteth the proud, and giveth grace to the humble.

Humble yourselves therefore under the mighty hand of God, that he may exalt you in due time.

1 Peter 5:5,6

When you set your will to fall upon the Rock, He will take out of you the stony heart. It will begin with the precious work of brokenness. What is it for? Brokenness is to break the outer in order that you may bring forth the beauty of the inner. If the outer has not been broken, we do not see the release of God's power. The issues of life are within the spirit man. It is when the release of the spirit comes that we find the release of the power. The power is in the Holy of Holies, but it must pass through the holy place to be made manifest in the outer court. It is in Gethsemane, the place of pressure, that we find the breaking of the vessel that will cause to pour forth the true anointing of God. The more a vessel is broken, the more the presence of God comes forth, and the quicker the Spirit moves through it.

We need to get delivered from the "pulpit mentality." We need to realize that, wherever we are, we are the dwelling place of God. Wherever we are and whatever He wants us to do, we should be on call, twenty-four hours a day. After having our souls dealt with and any areas of resistance to the Father's will wiped out, we should be tuned in to Him. Because we have fallen on the Rock, at any moment, we should be ready to release the flow of His presence. All of this comes through the saving of the soul.

When your soul is saved, you are released from the intimidation of witnessing to someone about Jesus. Laying hands on someone to bring healing in the supermarket will no longer make you nervous. When a manifestation of a word of knowledge comes to you about someone you've never met, you won't sit and reason it out trying to decide if that was God or you. When your soul is saved and in cooperation with the spirit man, he loves to see God move in your life.

It is only after your soul gets saved that you truly understand what it is to love yourself. You *can't* love yourself before the soul gets saved. The soul man is disgusting to be around. To truly love yourself is to love the work God has done in your soul and to appreciate the subservient role the soul now has in your life. The soul becomes a channel for the spirit to flow through rather than an obstacle for him to have to overcome.

6
THE SUPER SOUL

Some people think it is enough just to find out that they are soulish and deal with that, but we are going to see further insight from the Word that we can be *super soul*. Let's define our terms more fully. The Greek word for soul, *psuche*, is also translated "life" in certain instances. Another term for the soul is *psuchikos*, or "natural."

But the natural man (*psuchikos*) **receiveth not the things of the Spirit of God: for they are foolishness unto him: neither can he know them, because they are spiritually** (*pneumatikos*) **discerned.**

1 Corinthians 2:14

This verse tells us two things about the *psuchikos* man: He cannot receive the things of the Spirit, and he cannot know them. The *natural* man is soul-controlled and soul-ruled. The particular kind of person mentioned here is an unregenerate man, yet through further study of the words *psuchikos* and *psuche*, we find that the same characteristic can be involved in the life of a born-again person. He also can be ruled by his *psuche*. That is why the Word admonishes the "saving of the soul" so strongly. (See the previous chapter.)

The work of evangelism is not what we call soul-winning, but spirit-winning. When a person is born again, it is the spirit of man that is a partaker of the divine nature, the *zoe* life of God, but from the moment of the new birth, the process of soul-saving begins.

Another term used incorrectly, many times, is *supernatural*. To be supernatural, literally, would be a *super-psuche,* a super soul. We do not need to be supernatural. We need to be super-spiritual. We need to get over the intimidating connotation of super-spiritual. The soul loves to go toward the *super-psuchikos* but does not want the *super-pneumatikos*. I do understand what people mean when they say, "We need a supernatural move of God," in the sense of being a move from above or beyond the natural or material dimension in which we live, but in terms of mankind, it would be more scriptural to say we need a super-spiritual move of God.

The field of psychology and of the psyche deals with the soulish area of man. Psychology is from two words: *psuche,* the soul, and *logia,* the discourse. So actually, psychology is wrong as it is constituted today. It is called the study of the mind, but it is really the study of the soul and the discourse of the soulish realm — mind, will, and emotions.

What is the *only* thing that can separate the spirit and soul? Only the Word of God can bring about this separation, not psychology or psychiatry, nor doctors, theologians, nor pastors. *Only the Word of God can separate!* The Word brings the *merismos*. The Word is the most powerful force in the earth today to reveal human behavior in all its traits. Apart from the Word, you base your thinking on simple or natural observation that will bring confusion and misunderstanding. *Psychology ends up being the soul of one person probing the soul of another.*

One Nature: Two Lives

Now, let's consider some things about Adam and Eve. Much of theology is based around a concept of man having two natures. That doctrine was developed in order to explain why people sin after they are born again, but the truth is seen in Adam and in what God gave him.

> **And the Lord God formed man of the dust of the ground** (body)**, and breathed into his nostrils the breath of life** (spirit)**; and man became a living soul.**

Genesis 2:7

When God imparted the spirit into Adam's body, he became a *living soul,* which means a living personality, an individual unique in personality, style, etc. Every person has a uniqueness that is precious. Yet people can become deceived by that thought and become full of pride, thinking they are "really something." In proper perspective, this uniqueness is the beauty of God's creativity, not something for which we can, or should, take credit to ourselves.

The soul is the seat of man's personality, and each of us is different. We live through our personalities, however. Our clothes may look in some aspects the same, but there are variations that show distinctiveness. You wear your hair differently, for example, just because you want to be you. There is nothing wrong with that *unless* you get over into the *super soul* area — the area of developing self-image and the other things that go along with that, such as self-adoration, self-love, how to appreciate yourself more, ten ways you can better yourself. Little by little, that road leads into humanism and **ye shall be as gods** (Gen. 3:5).

Before Adam sinned, he had *one* nature, the nature of God, divine nature, but he had two lives — the life of the spirit *(zoe)* and the life of the soul *(psuche,* self-life). Jesus said that in the day you seek to save your *psuche*, you will lose it. Did Adam go with the *psuche* or the *zoe*? He went with the self-ruled life. When he sought to save it, he lost his *psuche*. In the process of choosing his soulish lifestyle, he lost. The *zoe* life of God left his spirit.

Before sin, Adam had one nature and two lives. He sinned and exchanged the divine nature for a sin nature. Adam still had one nature, but then he lost one life, zoe. The result was that Adam had only one life, self-life. By concept, Adam and Eve became dualistic — they had a sin nature and a self-ruled lifestyle. Selfishness motivated every decision. Sin became their nature, and *psuche* became their life. This was still the condition of humanity when Jesus came.

The Great Exchange

Jesus came as the Great Exchange. He was going to exchange life for life and nature for nature. He had to get back into man the divine nature and remove the sin nature. He had to get back into man the *zoe* or the life of the spirit, but He could not do that unless an exchange took place. We understand what He did. He bore our sins. He bore *our* sicknesses and diseases and anything else that went along with them. In fact, the reality is found in John 10:

I am the good shepherd: the good shepherd giveth his life (*psuche*) for the sheep.

As the Father knoweth me, even so know I the Father: and I lay down my life (*psuche*) for the sheep.

77

Therefore doth my Father love me, because I lay down my life *(psuche)*, **that I might take it again.**

John 10:11,15,17

What life did He give?

Yet it pleased the Lord to bruise him (this is prophetically referring to Jesus Christ); **he hath put him to grief: when thou shalt make his soul** *(nephesh,* Hebrew; *psuche,* Greek) **an offering for sin . . .** (Isa. 53:10). What became an offering for sin? His soul. Did He sin? No. He was *made* an offering for sin. The lamb in the Old Testament did not die because of its sin, nor did the Lamb of the New Testament.

. . . Thou shalt make his soul (not his spirit) **an offering for sin, he shall see his seed, he shall prolong his days, and the pleasure of the Lord shall prosper in his hand.**

He shall see of the travail of his soul, and shall be satisfied: by his knowledge shall my righteous servant justify many; for he shall bear their iniquities.

Therefore will I divide him a portion with the great, and he shall divide the spoil with the strong; because he hath poured out his soul *(nephesh)* **unto death . . . .**

Isaiah 53:10-12

The life of the flesh is in the blood, according to Leviticus 17:11: **For the life of the flesh is in the blood: and I have given it to you upon the altar to make an atonement for your souls: for it is the blood that maketh an atonement for the soul.** The word *life* used here is *nephesh.* The soulish life is in the blood, and it was His blood that was poured out. When you start

78

looking at redemption, you find that the terms "blood" and "soul" are synonymous.

Jesus said that He would lay down His life, *psuche*, self-life:

> **Even as the son of man came not to be ministered unto, but to minister, and to give his life** (*psuche*) **a ransom for many.**
>
> Matthew 20:28

> **Hereby perceive we the love of God, because he laid down his life** (*psuche*) **for us: and we ought to lay down our lives** (*psuche*) **for the brethren.**
>
> 1 John 3:16

So what did He give, His *pneuma*-spirit or His *psuche*-soul as an offering for sin? According to the Word, He laid down His *psuche*. Why? He laid down His self-life because that was what Adam took up in the Garden of Eden. When Adam chose the self-life, he lost the *zoe*-life of God. But when Jesus laid down His self-life, He brought back to mankind the *zoe*-life. He had to give up His *psuche* that you might have *zoe*.

> **I am come that they might have life** (*zoe*)**, and that they might have it more abundantly.**
>
> John 10:10b

> **And he bare the sin of many, and made intercession for the transgressors.**
>
> Isaiah 53:12d

When Adam sinned, he lost the *zoe* life. All he had left was a self-life and a sin-nature. When Jesus came and paid the price at Calvary, He provided righteousness for us and a new nature. Instantly, people could be born again and receive the divine nature, but it was obvious that the *psuche* was still around. The soul man needed to get into the Word and get dealt with. At the moment of being born again, man goes into a double-minded lifestyle, a manner of standing in two ways with two trees to partake of — the Tree of Life or the Tree of Knowledge of Good and Evil.

The Nature of the Soul

Let's look at the nature of the soul. Before Adam sinned, the initiation and motivation of his soul was the spirit man (*pneumatikos*). To understand *pneuma*, let's relate it to another modern term — the *pneumatic* tool, a wind- or air-driven tool. The force behind it is the air. If you separate the tool from the air, it becomes lifeless, not motivated. When Adam lost *zoe*, the life or breath of the spirit, and took from his soul the source of motivation, the soul man did not know what happened. He was without motivation because Adam's spirit had been in authority over his soul.

In the Garden, Adam's spirit declined. The soul man remained alive and active but now became aware of himself. Adam's soul became a personality with an introspective lifestyle that began a new world of self. What did Adam and Eve do to cover the exposure of their nakedness? They tried to cover it with fig leaves and aprons. Because the soul man needs some form of motivation, he looks elsewhere. The source he finds is *super-soul*.

The soul man still needs breath to motivate him, and what we call "psychic power" is the soul man finding breath from "another" spirit. Somebody is furnishing a driving wind for motivation and initiation to the soul. To us, as "Word people," clairvoyance, mental telepathy, extrasensory perception, mind projection, astral projection, palm reading, astrology, etc. are all obviously from another source than God. All of these are manifestations of evil spirits expressing their breath through a yielded *psuche,* and that is a *super-psuchikos* or the world of the supernatural.

Bridging — Merging — Blending

If you have ever given a prophesy that was not of God, you prophesied out of your soul. Who inspired or in-breathed that? You can tell when you are perceiving by the soul. It leaves an eerie presence in the place. It shuts down the *pneuma.* There can be words of knowledge or words of wisdom, Satan's counterfeits, that are from the super-soul. That is why Charismatics need to become more discerning. They could be in the forerunner stage of a super-soul and not even know it, because there is another move going on in the earth that is not of God. Its logo, or symbol, is the rainbow. Let me give you some basic information on that movement.

On one side of the rainbow is the word *personality* (man's soul). On the other side is the word *oversoul.* Members of the movement themselves say that Satan is the lord over the soul. When I began to get the revelation concerning the super-soul, I had no idea that they were usurping the rainbow, God's symbol, but here are three "words" the Lord gave me that are going to happen in Christendom in our generation, *unless* we get hold of the Word of God:

1. Satan is going to try to bridge the personality of man and link it to himself. *When I saw the rainbow, I knew that it was the bridge.*
2. He will try to merge the oversoul (his own personality) and the personality of man.

3. He will then blend them until they become one.

The Book of Revelation tells us where Satan's seat is, and it is neither heaven nor hell. The only place we find him seated is the soulish realm. Read the accounts of Jesus casting out demons. Every demon was expressing its personality through the life of that person and had robbed that person of his own personality. It had linked itself with the individual and had begun to merge the personality of the demonic spirit with the personality of the person. Once blended, the demonic personality being expressed canceled out the human personality. We say, "Well, that is just the way they are — moody," or whatever else, but it is really super-soul or oversoul.

Do Christians have super-souls? "Well, you know, God told me the other day . . . ." You had better check that "word" out closely before you do it, because sometimes it is what we want to do, hoping God will confirm it. On other occasions, it may be some other spirit than the Holy Spirit trying to get its will across, and you kind of liked the idea and went for it. That is a super-soul mentality. Many people have thought they heard from God in a certain area and later found out what they heard was demonically inspired.

The truth is that everyone has had that opportunity and has gone for it at some time. They were in the position that Paul spoke to Timothy about: **In meekness instructing those that oppose themselves . . .** (2 *Tim.* 2:25).

Super-Soul Moods

My wife has given me permission to share some of the things we have experienced through the years. When we first married, she was very moody. I could

82

get up in the morning, and there was a heaviness in our house. I would leave, have a great day, but when I came home, that heaviness was still there. I talked to her for two or three months about these moods, and she would just look at me and say, "Honey, *that's just the way I am*. I have always had these moods."

What she did not know was what I had already learned by that time. It is called "super-soul."

I told her, "That is *not* just the way you are, Gloria. You are a new creature, but your soul needs to be dealt with," and there we would go, just as you do, with "My mother was that way" or "It's just the Irish or the German (or whatever racial traits of which you are proudest)." She would bring up all these reasons why she was "that way," but what was it, in reality? The bridging, merging, and blending that she was emanating was the super-soul presence and personality. Through my wife, death was being released into our home, and she didn't even know it, nor did anyone else. That was just the way Gloria was, and everyone bought the deception, but I knew that was not "the way she was."

One day, I left the house to do some things. When I returned, she was standing at the kitchen sink washing dishes. The moment I stepped in, I perceived — not by psycho-analysis, but by the Spirit of God — that she was "in one of her moods."

I asked her, "How are you doing, Baby?"

"Fine," she said.

I said, "Been having a good day?"

"Yeah," she responded.

I bypassed every one of those lies and walked up to her. I laid my hands on her head and said, "I take authority over this foul spirit in the name of Jesus. Regardless of what Gloria calls it, I call it a work of the devil, and I command in the name of Jesus for it to depart from her and for this moodiness to depart from her in Jesus' name, from this day on. Get out of my house — **Now!**"

When I did that, she just stood there for a moment, then turned to me with a totally different countenance.

She asked, "What happened?"

I said, "Super-soul, that's what happened."

She said, "It was true, wasn't it?"

"Yes, honey," I replied, "It was."

From that moment on, she took a different look at these things I am teaching. She saw the need of a *merismos* in her life, a need to be able to determine where Satan had blended his personality into hers and hers into his where he could do whatever he wanted to. He could emanate death and cause problems and strife.

Understand me clearly: No church ever split just out of *psuche*. It always splits out of *super-soul*. It starts out of *psuche*, but it ends up with all kinds of super-soul help. The difference between mankind and demons is that we are eagles, and the demons are vultures. Vultures are always looking for a hunk of raw flesh. That is why they spend so much time soaring over churches. They are just waiting for someone's pride or ego to get offended and, when it does, that *psuche* will submit to super-soul assistance, which is witchcraft.

You can prove that is true when you start praying your curses over the Body of Christ or the man of God trying to run him out. You might as well get a doll and stick pins in it.

"I'll take authority over this and from now on this church will not grow any further. I'll get me about a dozen men and women, and we'll intercede, pray and fast, and bind and loose, and we'll have that carnal preacher who won't hear from God run out before the end of the week."

Here come the vultures. They have found some dead meat. Flesh is calling out to them to come and devour. It is super-soul time. This is when Christians get involved in strife and contention, anger and hostility, and think that is "just the way we are." I'll tell you right now that if you go over into strife, you will end up with all the assistance you need. Demons will teach you how to pray, to bind and loose, and to do things you never thought you could do. When all your witchcraft curses come to pass, if the recipient does not know how to stop them, then you stand back and say, "See there, I told you so."

7

THE OVERSOUL

Satan's major avenue of influence in the earth is through super-soul. Luke 9 shows us clearly the operation of it.

> And it came to pass, when the time was come that he should be received up, he stedfastly set his face to go to Jerusalem,

> And sent messengers before his face: and they went, and entered into a village of the Samaritans, to make ready for him.

> And they did not receive him, because his face was as though he would go to Jerusalem.

> And when his disciples James and John saw this, they said, Lord, wilt thou that we command fire to come down from heaven, and consume them, even as Elias did?

> But he turned, and rebuked them, and said, Ye know not what manner of spirit ye are of.

> For the Son of man is not come to destroy men's lives, but to save them. And they went to another village.

> **Luke 9:51-56**

Look closely at what Jesus said of James and John at that particular moment: Ye know not what manner of spirit ye are of. *What spirit were they of at the time? Super-soul! They were getting some assistance with that thought. "But, brother, it was just a little thought." You had better know how to be* **casting down imaginations, and every high thing that** *exalteth* **itself against the knowledge of God, and bringing into captivity every thought to the obedience of Christ** (2 Corinthians 10:5). There is a revelation right there. The soul always *exalts* itself **against the knowledge of God.**

One of the areas of confusion that Christians have fought over is whether a Christian can have a demon. There are two levels on which Satan can influence lives. Indirect influence is by planting a thought in your mind as corruptible seed that produces after its kind. If not dealt with, it will bring a harvest of death in its many manifestations. How does he do that? One way is through a teacher, often behind a pulpit, sowing the thought in your mind — false teaching. He leaves it, and you live it. The other way is direct influence, and that is where the demonic spirit begins to live through your personality.

The five "I will's" of Isaiah 14 reveal Satan's intentions in and through a person's life, his desire to absorb a person's personality and manifest his own.

> **How art thou fallen from heaven, O Lucifer, son of the morning! how art thou cut down to the ground, which didst weaken the nations!**
>
> **For thou hast said in thine heart,**
> *I will* **ascend into heaven** (self-exaltation)
>
> *I will* **exalt my throne above the stars of God:** (power exaltation)
>
> *I will* **sit also upon the mount of the congregation, in the sides of the north:** (wanting an equality with the hierarchy of heaven)
>
> *I will* **ascend above the heights of the clouds;** *(I'm going to surpass them all!)*
>
> *I will* **be like the most High.**
> **Isaiah 14:12-14**

God wants your soul, and Satan wants your soul. Satan wants to be lord over the soul. The word *over-soul* means "Satan, lord over the soul."

What do you think is happening when thoughts come to you like this: "Boy, I'm terrific. I am one of the greatest men of God in the earth today. The world is just waiting for me. Why haven't they discovered me any sooner? I should be leading the praise and worship. They obviously have not heard my voice." That is super-soul: self-awareness backed by a demonic presence boasting, bragging, and pumping you up so that *he* can take over through you.

Satan's Use of Soul Power

Satan has plans for the soul of man. He desires control over the soul to use as a pawn to bring dominance over the earth. He has no kingdom to be a king over. He is not a king. When God expelled him from Heaven, he was cast down to earth. Heaven is not his kingdom, earth is not his kingdom, and Hell is not his kingdom. Heaven is the Lord's, earth is man's, and Hell is an eternal prison for Satan, his angels, and the wicked. Therefore, Satan can only rule and reign through the subjection of man's soul on earth.

Satanic principalities and powers influence humanity through man's thought processes, imaginations, dreams, and desires. This is the reason for the world of parapsychology and supernatural phenomena in the earth today. Demonic activity comes through all the "psychic," or supernatural, manifestations, such as hypnotism, magic, familiar spirits, levitation, and so forth. America has been invaded by the world of psychic forces and super-soul. All of this is Satan using men's souls. This is where man's personality is being altered and changed. Satan is the Oversoul, lord over the soul.

He is using the souls of mankind to perform demonic signs and wonders and to bring counterfeit works of the Holy Spirit. His objective is to use mankind, God's creation, as puppets against God. The mystery of iniquity already is at work. (2 Thess. 2:7.) Satan is bridging, merging, and blending the personality of man to his own. Satan has encountered the soul, and it has become his throne, but his kingdom expands only to the degree that an individual surrenders his soul. Mankind does not realize that he has become a pawn and puppet in the hands of the master of the psychic.

God's Word condemns the world of psychic involvements.

> **Regard not them that have familiar spirits, neither seek after wizards, to be defiled by them: I am the Lord your God.**
>
> **Leviticus 19:31**

> **And the soul that turneth after such as have familiar spirits, and after wizards, to go a whoring after them, I will even set my face against that soul, and will cut him off from among his people.**
>
> **Leviticus 20:6**

> **A man also or woman that hath a familiar spirit, or that is a wizard, shall surely be put to death: they shall stone them with stones: their blood shall be upon them.**
>
> **Leviticus 20:27**

When thou art come into the land which the Lord thy God giveth thee, thou shalt not learn to do after the abominations of those nations.

There shall not be found among you any one that maketh his son or his daughter to pass through the fire, or that useth divination, or an observer of times, or an enchanter, or a witch,

Or a charmer, or a consulter with familiar spirits, or a wizard, or a necromancer.

For all that do these things are an abomination unto the Lord: and because of these abominations the Lord thy God doth drive them out from before thee.

Thou shalt be perfect with the Lord thy God.

For these nations, which thou shalt possess, hearkened unto observers of times, and unto diviners: but as for thee, the Lord thy God hath not suffered thee so to do.

Deuteronomy 18:9-14

Therefore shall evil come upon thee; thou shalt not know from whence it riseth: and mischief shall fall upon thee; thou shalt not be able to put it off: and desolation shall come upon thee suddenly, which thou shalt not know.

Stand now with thine enchantments, and with the multitude of thy sorceries, wherein thou hast laboured from thy youth; if so be thou shalt be able to profit, if so be thou mayest prevail.

Thou art wearied in the multitude of thy counsels. Let now the astrologers, the stargazers, the monthly prognosticators, stand up, and save thee from these things that shall come upon thee.

Behold, they shall be as stubble; the fire shall burn them; they shall not deliver themselves from the power of the flame: there shall not be a coal to warm at, nor fire to sit before it.

Isaiah 47:11-14

God has not changed. His Word has not changed. These things that are being done in America are still an abomination to God, but Satan's five "I will's" of Isaiah 14 can only be fulfilled through man's will.

Neither yield ye your members as instruments of unrighteousness unto sin: but yield yourselves unto God, as those that are alive from the dead, and your members as instruments of righteousness unto God.

Romans 6:13

And it came to pass, as we went to prayer, a certain damsel possessed with a spirit of divination met us, which brought her masters much gain by soothsaying:

The same followed Paul and us, and cried, saying, These men are the servants of the most high God, which shew unto us the way of salvation.

And this did she many days. But Paul, being grieved, turned and said to the spirit, I command thee in the name of Jesus Christ to come out of her. And he came out the same hour.

Acts 16:16-18

91

Here is a prophecy that would likely be accepted in any charismatic fellowship. Everything she said was true, but what was the source? Where was that demonic spirit operating from? It was operating from the woman's soul. It took revelation from the Spirit of God to uncover it. Was she right in what she said? It sounded like a good prophecy and was very accurate as to content. There was only one problem — super-soul!

If you do not get an overseer to your soul, you will be victimized by super-soul. You may not want it, and you may want to deny it, but your soul will appreciate the right spiritual authority over it. Jesus has provided bishops as overseers of the souls of God's people. He also has given you a local body to which you may submit. The main reason Adam and Eve blew it was because Adam refused to bring oversight to his own soul and failed to provide oversight to his wife's soul. As a result, they submitted to the wrong spirit.

The reborn human spirit, that new creature in Christ Jesus, is to be the source of oversight to your soul. It is from the spirit that breath is released to motivate and initiate the soul. We need no other energy, not Satan's and not self's. We do not need to pump ourselves up by super-soul. Super-soul wants to be like the Most High God, to take the concepts of God, adapt them to self, and operate them as God.

You say, "But it's not so obvious."

It's obvious when you begin to undergo the *merismos!* You can see it is nothing more than Satan's rebellion modernized and packaged, although it is called *humanism.* Let's look at another scripture in Acts.

But a certain man named Ananias, with Sapphira his wife, sold a possession,

And kept back part of the price, his wife also being privy to it, and brought a certain part, and laid it at the apostles' feet.

But Peter said, "Ananias, why hath Satan filled thine heart to lie to the Holy Ghost, and to keep back part of the price of the land?

Whiles it remained, was it not thine own? and after it was sold, was it not in thine own power? why hast thou conceived this thing in thine heart? thou hast not lied unto men, but unto God.

Acts 5:1-4

Where did Ananias and Sapphira get the thought to lie to the Holy Ghost? *Super-soul.* They had assistance — a little thought. One Bible teacher tried to use this to prove that the devil can possess a Christian, but the Scripture did not say they were "possessed" of a demon. Peter said Satan had filled their hearts with a lie. It was conceived by giving place to a thought.

Paul *merismosed* the difference between something that came from the spirit and something that came from the soul. Peter *merismosed* the difference, and Jesus, "the *Merismos* Man," knew when it came out of the spirit and when it came out of the soul. The joy of this is that *you* can become *merismosed* to the degree that you can know what comes from the spirit and what comes from the soul.

People are easily impressed by gifts and manifestations of the Holy Spirit, but these have nothing to do with character development. We must learn to make a *merismos*. Listen to what Jesus said when the disciples returned excited about the move of power in healing the sick and casting out devils:

Notwithstanding, in this rejoice not, that the spirits are subject unto you; but rather rejoice, because your names are written in heaven.

Luke 10:20

From that time forth began Jesus to shew unto his disciples, how that he must go unto Jerusalem, and suffer many things of the elders and chief priests and scribes, and be killed, and be raised again the third day.

Then Peter took him, and began to rebuke him, saying, Be it far from thee, Lord: This shall not be unto thee.

Matthew 16:21,22

In the margin of my Bible, it gives me the Greek for this. Peter turned to Jesus and said, "Pity thyself." Jesus has told them what is about to happen, the suffering, dying, and resurrection, but Peter said, "Wait a minute, Jesus, think about yourself. You don't have to do that. Just think about good old number one. I mean, it's just the natural thing to do."

But he turned, and said unto Peter, Get thee behind me, Satan: thou art an offence unto me: for thou savourest (thoughts and mentality) **not the things that be of God, but those that be of men.**

Matthew 16:23

Two guys are walking down the street together. One says, "I've got to go over to such and such a place and minister to a person." The other says, "Oh, you don't have to do that." Super-soul!

What happened between Peter and Jesus was demonically inspired through the soul man of Peter.

Right up to the Garden of Gethsemane where he pulled the sword, Peter had that same spirit working through him and thought he was doing God a favor.

Saul of Tarsus, super-soul, killed Christians, thinking he was doing God a favor. Who inspired it? "Oh, that was just the way Saul was. Those Israelites are sometimes hot tempered." No, it was super-soul! It was Satan's use of Saul's soul.

Unless your spirit takes the oversight, your soul man will be looking for motivation from some other source, and he will find it. He likes the spirit-thrust in your life.

The Beginning of Super-Soul

James 3:15 says, **This wisdom descendeth not from above, but is earthly, sensual, devilish.** The word *sensual* in the Greek is *psuchikos*. The sensual man is the soulish man. The soul is sandwiched between that which is earthly and that which is demonic. The soul is influenced by earthly overtones and demonic influences. Therefore, the soul must be saved by the engrafted Word, or it will eventually become subject to both the *kosmos* lifestyle and the demonic lifestyle.

In the Garden of Eden, God planted two trees and commanded Adam and Eve not to eat of one of those trees, warning them of death to follow in the day they ate of it. Immediately following God's command, we find the serpent tempting Adam and Eve to disobey God by promising them two things: that they would be as gods and that they would not die.

These Satanic promises hold the concepts that through the process of death and rebirth, one can continue to progress unto the superior level of a god.

Satan is still promising humanity this today through many religions and cults.

The soul chooses to disobey God and partake of the Tree of Knowledge of Good and Evil. Although the tree is called *good* and *evil*, it is still the same tree producing the same fruit — death. We are commanded of God not to choose that tree. To choose for your own life what is right and wrong is to deny the choice of God for your life. Therefore, you set yourself up as god over your life and begin the pursuit of a self-indulging lifestyle. Perhaps because you are a Christian, you would not choose the road of evil. You would not steal, cheat, rob, or destroy, but the results are the same for the *good* chosen by the soul because *it is the same tree.* That choice may be good, but it is not God. That one letter of difference between *God* and *good* can cost you your life.

God has commanded us not to choose what is right for our own lives. Many choose where they will live, what vocation they want, what church to go to, what they want for their lives, but the choice is not ours to make. Go to the Tree of Life and find out what God has already chosen for your life. Find out what God wants you to do, where He wants you to live, and what church He wants you to attend.

It is time to obey God's first commandment and stop partaking of the Tree of Knowledge of Good and Evil. That tree is the soul's choice. Allow the spirit man to have preeminence and follow after the Way of Life.

Beware of Satan's promise that says, "Let us make God in our own image and after our own likeness."

8
METAMORPHOSIS
OF THE MIND

We have seen in the *merismos* that there is a *separation for clarification*. There are times when it may look as if the soul man is worthless and useless, but we are going to see that after he is dealt with, he can be very beautiful and cooperative. In other words, there comes the *unification for cooperation*. We will see how he can be profitable and what an asset the soul man can be. The soul in proper alignment is a powerful tool.

The extreme of "the-old-man-must-be-crucified" teaching is to spend a lifetime crucifying yourself and never live the resurrected life. There is a way to live the resurrected life with the soul man having reckoned himself to be dead to himself but alive unto God.

Wherefore lay aside all filthiness and superfluity of naughtiness, and receive with meekness the engrafted word, which is able to save your souls.

James 1:21

The only thing able to save your soul is the engrafted Word of God. It is the key to saving the mind, will, and emotions. However, the Word deals differently with each of those areas. It is the same Word, but there is a difference in its operations.

The work of the Word in the mind is called "the renewing of the mind." God renews the thought processes.

The way God saves the will is through your denial of yourself. The Word speaks of a continual denial of the will of a man to move independently of God, giving the will no right to speak independently of Christ. *We are already dead.* We are not trying to kill ourselves or break our will. We live on the fact that the will has *already* been dealt with. The power that kept your mind and will captivated and controlled your emotions was broken. Now you must deny your will the right to move independently of God. Deny the will with the forces of the Word by reminding the soul that he has been crucified with Christ.

In dealing with the emotions, it is a training process, a re-programming. Hebrews 5 deals with the saving of the emotions.

> **For every one that useth milk is unskillful in the word of righteousness: for he is a babe.**
>
> **But strong meat belongeth to them that are of full age, even those who by reason of use have their senses exercised to discern both good and evil.**

> **Hebrews 5:13,14**

You must get into the meat of God's Word. You must become a master of the Sword. You become skillful in the use of the Word against the senses through practice. You direct your senses to go with the Word of God when they want to go independently of the Word. For example, 1 Peter 2:24 says, . . . **By whose stripes ye** *were* **healed.** When our bodies say we are sick, we have been taught to save our senses and bring them in line with the Word by not being moved by what we see or feel. Through practice at doing this, we can retrain our senses to correlate with the Word. We can speak to our bodies and call them into line with what God has said.

I am not moved by emotions or depression. I have joy. Frustrations will not dominate me for I have victory in Jesus' name. Regardless of the circumstances that I hear and see, I am more than a conqueror. Your emotions are fed by the physical senses and they bring the will into involvement with them. You must save them by the Word!

Be Ye Transformed

Let's look now at an area of the saving of the soul called *metamorphosis of the mind*. There has been a great push of the Spirit in this area, because it is in the mental realm where Satan begins to take control of the soul. He wants your mind. His method is to sow corruptible seeds into your thought processes which will train you to respond to his lifestyle. (I have a 4-tape series, "Root of the Problem," which deals with this area in greater depth.)

There are both direct and indirect demonic influences. The direct influence is dealt with by using your authority in Jesus to resist the demonic spirit. The indirect influence is the wrong teaching and unbelief that has been sown in your thinking. The teacher leaves, but the teaching remains. In dealing with the indirect influence, you have to go into your mental realm and, by the power of the Word of God, root out that corruptible seed and exchange it with an incorruptible seed. Those thoughts have to be plucked out of the mind.

Often the "plucking out" process is very difficult because once the thought is accepted, it moves over into the realm of the will. You have purpose, intent, desire, and, at that point, you are determined that what you think is true, and that makes you hard to deal with. Thought has changed to belief, and you identify with the belief. It is a part of you, and any effort to change that belief feels, many times, like an attack. It takes a real merismos, a real "dividing asunder," to get you to see the truth so that you can be delivered from the counterfeit or the false.

Only the Word of God, the engrafted Word, is able to save the soul. When you get into the thought processes to change your thinking, it takes more than just being exposed to the Word because of the resistance of the will and emotions to any changing of the mind. You must take the *engrafted Word* and embed or implant it in a permanent fixed position in your mind. By dwelling on the Word through meditation, you become the product of the Word by God's power of transformation.

Revelation — Transfiguration — Manifestation

The Word works on three levels: thirtyfold, sixtyfold, and a hundredfold. (Matt. 13:23.) It is also called the blade, the ear, and the full corn in the ear. (Mark 4:26-29.) We see that the dealings of the Word are progressive, and so it is with the saving of the soul. It is not instantaneous as is the new birth. The good, acceptable, and perfect will of God is found in all three stages, but let's look at three other words that describe what occurs any time you approach the Word of God in areas where it operates as a process. They are *revelation*, *transfiguration*, and *manifestation*.

The first thing that happens when the Word of God comes to you is *revelation*. It reveals its truth. The more you attend to the Word, the quicker it takes you to *transfiguration*. The Word revealed begins the work of transforming you. It deals with your thinking, attitudes, personality, and behavior. It affects and changes your life. As it continues its course, it will take you to *manifestation*, which means you are then able to say, **"The Word was made flesh, and dwelt among us"** (John 1:14).

At that point, you no longer have just a revelation of the Word. The process of change has brought you to a place where the Word has become a lifestyle. You are in the Word, and the Word is in you, and you are one. You become the manifestation of that teaching.

> **I beseech you therefore, brethren, by the mercies of God, that ye present your bodies a living sacrifice, holy, acceptable unto God, which is your reasonable service.**
>
> **And be not conformed to this world: but be ye transformed** (metamorphoo) **by the renewing of your mind . . . .**

Romans 12:1,2

For what purpose does this metamorphosis come? **That ye may prove what is that good, and acceptable, and perfect, will of God** (Rom. 12:2c).

Many people are walking in the *good* will of God. Others walk in the *acceptable,* but you can walk in the *perfect* will of God for your life. You no longer speak of yourself, but you now speak the Words of God. You no longer do your own will but the will of the Father. You have received the commandment of what to speak and what to do. Jesus never moved or spoke independently of the Father. You can walk in the realm that fulfills the order of God. It is the manifested realm of God in your life, but before you get there, you must go through a revelation and a transfiguration.

In the light of this, look at 2 Corinthians 3:18: **But we all, with open face beholding as in a glass the glory of the Lord, are changed into the same image from glory to glory, even as by the Spirit of the Lord.** Changed! How? We are changed from *glory* to *glory!* It is a progression from one stage of glory to another to another. There is a level of glory in revelation. There is another level in transfiguration and yet a higher level in manifestation.

When you become a son who manifests the glory of God through your life, you have dealt with your soul. You no longer move in that area independently of God. You are no longer quick with opinions, views, and ideas. All the times you just spoke your mind, or said what you felt, no longer occur. You are coming into maturity. Your body is under control. Your mind, will, and emotions have been dealt with by God, and the spirit man is in ascendancy over them. God can now trust you with His power. He can bring presence and glory through you as His vessel.

The word *change* in 2 Corinthians 3:18 is the same Greek word, *metamorphoo,* which is used in Romans 12:2 and translated "transformed." **And be not conformed to this world: but be ye transformed** *(metamorphoo)* . . . .

A "metamorphosis" is a transformation of a person's lifestyle according to its association. It is not just change for change's sake. It is change according to its association. When the term was adapted from Greek to English, there was little, if any, alteration in its true meaning. An example of metamorphosis is the transformation of a caterpillar into a butterfly. It is a progressive change from a lower to a higher life. The soul begins as a caterpillar but comes out a magnificent butterfly.

God has placed in this earth the principle of metamorphosis. At the new birth, we had an instant transformation. We put off the old nature and put on the new — instantly! The soul, however, goes through a progression. Let's break down the term *metamorphosis* and look at its parts. *Meta* means "to be modified according to association." *Morphoo* means "to be changed, fashioned, or transformed into." *Metamorphosis* is a change as the result of something — *a change through association*.

You must associate *with* something in order to be changed *like* something. Those with whom you associate will bring a change to your life. That is why it is so important to choose the proper associations. Hook up with God to be changed into His image and likeness through His Word. The Word will change you according to His personality, nature, and lifestyle. God's Word is full of His attributes. Become an exact duplication of His kind by the changing of your thought processes by the Word.

All the areas of the mental must be transformed or there will not be a free flowing of God's life. All the reasonings, logics, and imaginations are to be changed. You must reason as God reasons and have God's logic and His imaginations.

"Be Not Conformed"

Let us see the word *conformed* for a moment. It is the Greek word *susche-matizo* from the root *psuche*. In 2 Corinthians 3:18, Paul was saying, "Do not associate with the soulish aspects of this world. Do not be fashioned by the soulish powers or unify yourself with the mentality, logic, reasoning, will, intent, purpose, or senses of humanity. Do not be twisted around with their deceptive technique, but break from the association of the world by associating with God's Word."

If you associate with religion, you will just become religious. However, we should not want religious change, but God's change in our lives. We should not be interested in new denominations, creeds, and doctrines apart from the will of God.

In the 60s, the hippies rebelled against the establishment saying they did not want "to conform," but what did they do in trying to seek uniqueness? They all "conformed" to each other and ended up all looking the same. What did they do? They found a world order and fashioned themselves around it, and all of them became clones of that order.

The way of God is not to suppress your personality. He desires individuality, variety, and for you to be unique, but He wants those areas of *psuche* that are contrary to Him changed so that His life can flow through the personality.

There are five terms that lay before us the concept of influence and change. They are: source, knowledge, thinking, belief, and confession. Let's take it progressively backwards to show each stage clearly in relationship to the others. A man's confession is the product of his belief. His belief is the result of his thinking. His thinking is the result of his knowledge, and his knowledge is the result of his source. The strength of the thought process is sandwiched in between the knowledge and the belief. In other words, drawing upon one of the sources of knowledge, God or Satan, shapes my thinking. One source says, "You are sick," but the other says, "By Jesus' stripes you were healed 2,000 years ago." (1 Pet. 2:24.)

Whichever source you draw knowledge from begins to set in motion the thought processes. If you will receive with meekness the engrafted Word, you will humble yourself to it immediately and believe it. If you choose not to, however, you will rationalize it on the basis of your knowledge of past experience, wrong teaching, views, and opinions that will formulate a belief that is inconsistent with scripture, and once you do, you will begin to speak your belief. Jesus said in Mark 11:23 that you have what you say, *believing:*

> **For verily I say unto you, That whosoever shall say unto this mountain, Be thou removed, and be thou cast into the sea; and shall not doubt in his heart, but shall believe that those things which he saith shall come to pass; he shall have whatsoever he saith.**

Once I hear you speak, I know from what source you are receiving. If your words do not line up with God's, directly or indirectly, you are drawing from Satan. **This wisdom descendeth not from above, but is earthly, sensual, devilish** (James 3:15). Do you remember that the Greek word for *sensual* is *psuchikos?* Whether directly or indirectly, Satan stands on either side of the soul, desiring entrance for the purpose of changing you into his image and likeness, to merge you with his personality, behavior, and thought processes, so that you will manifest his desires.

The problem is not just in giving place to a bad thought. The problem is what you become by a process of association over a period of time. It will place you into a position of opposition to the truth. You have submitted to Satan and are resisting God by resisting His Word. A prime example of people who do that are those who preach that speaking in tongues is of the devil. They stand in opposition to the truth of God.

For an example, suppose you are one of those people. The process works like this: Your source, being Satan, has all of a sudden given you knowledge that provoked your thinking. You finally come to a certain belief against speaking in tongues based on the accumulation of facts from what you have heard and the books you have read against tongues. You agreed with the thought, you believed it, so you began to acknowledge the false teaching by your words — "tongues are of the devil." The problem, however, goes even further. Your belief is not a passive thing. It will lead you to attack the work of God if it is presented to you. You then have become anti-Word, which is anti-Christ, although you may be born again.

God, of course, wants your mental realm even more than Satan does because He loves you and wants the best for you, while Satan wants to use you for his own purposes. God's desire is for the mind, will, and emotional functions to check in with the Word of God before making a move. As I said before, at times it may appear to people, as they become involved in the teaching of *merismos*, that the soul is worthless or useless, but the emphasis is on the hope set before us, not just on the position the soul has held. Once the soul man is dealt with by God, his wrong strengths are broken, and he is brought back into proper position as an assistant to the spirit man for releasing the life of the spirit.

By using the engrafted Word, a metamorphosis occurs in your thinking. Matthew 17:1,2 shows the power of the work of metamorphosis:

And after six days Jesus taketh Peter, James, and John his brother, and bringeth them up into an high mountain apart,

And was transfigured before them: and his face did shine as the sun, and his raiment was white as the light.

The word *transfigured* is the Greek word *metamorphoo*. Three times we have found this word in the original. It has been translated "transformed," "changed," and "transfigured," but all three translated words mean the same thing.

Look at the power of *metamorphoo* in the life of Jesus. . . . **And his face did shine as the sun, and his raiment was white as the light.** It actually changed his clothing. The work of a metamorphosis will bring an unveiling and a release of the glory to where you will emanate the very presence of God's glory. You will never be the same again. You'll never live like you used to live.

Pulling Down Strongholds

We need to make a distinction between the thought process and the reasoning process for the purpose of clarification. The thought process is that which begins to formulate reasonings. We are to recapture our thoughts and pull down our imaginations.

For though we walk in the flesh, we do not war after the flesh:

(For the weapons of our warfare are not carnal, but mighty through God to the pulling down of strongholds;)

Casting down imaginations, and every high thing that exalteth itself against the knowledge of God, and bringing into captivity every thought to the obedience of Christ.

2 Corinthians 10:3-5

The phrase **pulling down strongholds** deals with things that need to be pulled down in our thought processes. The word *imaginations* also is the same word translated as "reasonings." Paul says what you must do is cast down reasonings and then bring thoughts into captivity.

During the process of waiting on God, when He begins to order or reorder a life, He will begin to lay it out before you. You then have questions such as this: "What is happening? What is going on? What is He doing?" Nothing seems to be taking place. With all the things He has promised and said, nothing seems to be happening. You have to watch your thought processes during this period and bring them into captivity. Otherwise, the thoughts will begin to develop into patterns.

The pattern-type of thinking is called the *noema*. The same word is used for Satan's "devices." It is a thought pattern or process that has plans or purposes in it. It is a kind of process that begins to formulate and develop reasonings, which are what Paul says must be pulled down. Reasoning is one of the hardest areas we encounter. The words *high thing* can be correlated in modern terminology to "skyscrapers." **Every high thing that exalteth itself.**

Let's say I have a thought process which is fertile (active and working). It has not been brought into captivity. It is running without reins and has not been captured by Christ. As a result, when I think in certain patterns, the *noemas* begin to formulate in my mind. If I do not begin to bring that process into captivity when it is just a thought and align it with the Word of God, it will begin to fabricate, or weave, a reasoning. The moment a reasoning is established, it becomes a fortified high skyscraper or high wall in front of my reasonings.

If I don't watch out, once I have fabricated and accepted that reasoning, I will establish that "building process" as a means in which I have confidence or trust. I will believe in that from then on. When the next thought comes, I will fabricate it into another fortified city or wall of defense in front of my thought processes. Multiply that ten or twelve times and you find your entire thought processes, your mind, has been blockaded by a defense or a fenced city called a "stronghold."

When you meet Jesus, a *metamorphosis* of the mind begins. He begins to tear down those strongholds by the Word of God and remove all those wrong reasonings and illogical conclusions. You begin to be greatly challenged by the power of the Word. Jeremiah says that the Word is like a hammer. (Jer. 23:29.) What the Word begins to do is flatten those reasonings and strongholds and to recapture your thought processes.

Let's say you are in a lull in your life, in a situation where you are just waiting on God to initiate something. You spend the entire evening before the Father trying to get direction, but nothing is being said. There is just silence, and you're "on hold." God is not communicating with you. Well, we don't panic because we have learned to trust God. It's no big deal. He knows what He is doing. Everything is under control.

If you don't know this, however, reasonings run away with you. The thoughts begin to fabricate reasonings, which become illogical or unscriptural, and they begin to establish strongholds. Your reasonings then begin to blame God, to criticize and murmur and say, "Why? How come? What's happening?" These are fabricating strongholds that will take tremendous power of God to destroy.

You need to learn two things: One is to pull down every form of reasoning that is contrary or exalts itself against God's Word; then, you bring into captivity every thought so that it does not keep on fabricating. Otherwise, your reasoning says, "Well, I tell you what, nothing's going on. I'm going to do something." You are about to make a mistake. If you do something before you hear, you're going to blow it. Ninety-nine and three-quarters percent of the time, that thought of what to do is not God, and it is going to bring death and destruction and cost you in some area.

I have been involved in "Ishmaels," and so have you. You must cast down these reasonings that can bring you into the work of the flesh. I am going to show you how to do this. First, you take the Word of God as your exalted final authority. You sift every thought through that channel called "the Word." Let the Word fabricate the reasonings because then they will be right reasonings. If it is improper, pull that reasoning down, capture it, and say, "No." If you learn to capture it quickly, it will not even fabricate. As long as you keep it in captivity, it will not reproduce wrong reasonings.

Reasonings are the hardest things to pull down and destroy in people's lives. Some of you had wrong reasonings just a few years ago concerning God's will for your lives. At one time, some of you had terrible reasonings on healing. Some of you may still have that fortified wall of reasoning that says, "Well, it is not God's will to heal everybody." That is a wrong reasoning because it is unscriptural and it will keep healing from getting through to you. That reasoning has to be torn down in order for you to have a receptive heart to the Holy Spirit and to receive the promises of God.

There are so many things in which these strongholds have stopped the word and will of God.

The Renewing of Your Mind

Everyone who meets Jesus needs to be exposed to a new way of thinking, not to a religious way of thinking, or an opinionated way of thinking, or to a denomination's way of thinking, but to the way that the Word thinks. We want the mind of Christ.

And be renewed in the spirit of your mind;

And that ye put on the new man, which after God is created in righteousness and true holiness.

Ephesians 4:23,24

Here we find a renewal of the spirit (or the attitudes) of the mind, a transfiguration that comes by a renewal of thinking and lifestyle. The Greek word for *renewed* is *ananeoo. Ana* means "up" or "reversal." *Neos* means "a newness or a freshness." It means a new lifestyle, a new way of living, a fresh way of thinking, a fresh attitude. This comes about by a work of God's Word.

Therefore we are buried with him by baptism into death: that like as Christ was raised up from the dead by the glory of the Father, even so we also should walk in newness of life.

Romans 6:4

"Newness" in the Greek is *kainotes.* It also means "freshness." Being exposed to and united with the Word will keep you fresh and new in the things of God. One of the real problems I have seen in ministries is when they stop giving fresh bread and hand out day-old "manna." It is a stale lifestyle.

111

Christians who become lethargic and apathetic are those who are not walking in the newness or freshness of life. They become stale because they have separated themselves from that which keeps them fresh, alive, and energetic every day. This is a perfect example of what happens to a garden that is not properly watered. It withers and dies. We need the dew of God upon our lives to keep us fresh, revived, and alive. Spending time each day with God in prayer and in His Word will act like dew upon your spirit and mind. You will not have to talk about what God did in your life 40 years ago. You can talk about right now because of the fresh move of God that is going on.

The mind not only needs this "watering," it *must* have it, or it will get bored and begin to look elsewhere for freshness. We want fresh "wonderbread," not day-old bread. Keep up to date with Jesus. People will want to be around you and to fellowship with you. You will be able to take that freshness and impart it to others.

Renewing — Cleansing — Preserving

In the work of *metamorphosis,* there are three words that reveal the secrets to its working. They are found first in Romans 12:2 where the word *renew* is used: **But be ye transformed by the *renewing* of your mind.** We have just discussed that aspect in the light of "freshness."

The second aspect is found in Ephesians 5:26: **That he might sanctify and cleanse it with the *washing* of water by the word.** What Paul is saying is that the Body of Christ needs a literal "brain washing" by the water of the Word to purge, cleanse, and purify our minds. The water of the Word will remove all the debris and overtones of the *psuche* lifestyle and act as a purifier.

112

The third word, or aspect, is in 1 Thessalonians 5:23: **And the very God of peace sanctify you wholly; and I pray God your whole spirit and soul and body be** *preserved* **blameless unto the coming of our Lord Jesus Christ.** The final work is one of preserving.

A lot of women can their own fruits, vegetables, jams, and jellies. When they make strawberry preserves, they do not get the old strawberries, but the fresh. Fresh berries make the best preserves. The second step, after getting the berries, is to wash them thoroughly, getting out all of the impurities so that nothing taints the taste of the fruit. The third step is to preserve them.

The reason for preserving can be compared to the programming of a computer. It enables you to transmit the same taste, or the same information, on a consistent basis each time a demand is made for it. For example, if you have been taught the proper alignment is "spirit, soul, and body," and someone says, "body, soul, and spirit," there is an immediate reaction. This occurs because you have been programmed and "preserved" in the way of thinking that spirit is first, then soul, and the body. You have apostolically aligned these elements in proper order. The reason for the reaction is that you have become a stickler for the Word. You want accuracy, not overtones. You want the freshness of the fruit and not the impurities of wrong teaching. You want proper order, the order of God's Word.

The way of God is to take each area of your life and, by His Word, renew you, wash you. He will preserve you in that, then go on to the next area, from "glory to glory," to bring about the metamorphosis of the mind. When that comes, you will have gone from revelation to transfiguration to manifestation. If you preserve before the right time, however, the truth is preserved with a lot of debris and is not "edible." It just doesn't taste right in your mouth.

God wants us to become preserved, or sealed, in the revelation of His Word so that we are immovable and unshakable, sanctified wholly. Your life is only as productive as the freshness of your walk with God. Keep a fresh word from God in your life:

And be renewed in the spirit of your mind;

And that ye put on the new man, which after God is created in righteousness and true holiness.

Ephesians 4:23,24

When we become transfigured, we become unpersuadable by counterfeits or lies. No one can talk us out of our victorious lifestyle. We are not moved by circumstances or opposition because we will then be **fully persuaded that, what he had promised, he was able also to perform** (Rom. 4:21). What God has said is now absolute truth and final authority. There is no compromising it or your position on it. You have been transfigured, and the glory of God is evidenced in your life.

9

GETHSEMANE: THE WINE PRESS

Jesus is the *Merismos* Man. He is the Word that divides and separates. By His very presence, there would be an exposure of what is spirit and what is soul, but let us look at something that the *Merismos* Man encountered that has been taken out of context and misunderstood. Let's look at what happened in the Garden of Gethsemane in the light of a work of *merismos*, because that is what really happened there.

Then cometh Jesus with them unto a place called Gethsemane, and saith unto the disciples, Sit ye here, while I go and pray yonder.

And he took with him Peter and the two sons of Zebedee, and began to be sorrowful and very heavy.

Then saith he unto them, My soul is exceeding sorrowful, even unto death: tarry ye here, and watch with me.

And he went a little further, and fell on his face, and prayed, saying, O my Father, if it be possible, let this cup pass from me: nevertheless, not as I will, but as thou wilt.

And he cometh unto the disciples, and findeth them asleep, and saith unto Peter, What, could ye not watch with me one hour?

Watch and pray, that ye enter not into temptation: the spirit indeed is willing, but the flesh is weak.

He went away again the second time, and prayed, saying, O my Father, if this cup may not pass away from me, except I drink it, thy will be done.

And he came and found them asleep again: for their eyes were heavy.

And he left them, and went away again, and prayed the third time, saying the same words.

Then cometh he to his disciples, and saith unto them, Sleep on now, and take your rest: behold, the hour is at hand, and the Son of man is betrayed into the hands of sinners.

Rise, let us be going: behold, he is at hand that doth betray me.

Matthew 26:36-46

I want to present to you what Jesus Christ really experienced in Gethsemane.

One of the teachings that has been presented from this chapter of Matthew is in the area of prayer: "If it be Thy will, Lord. Thy will be done, not mine." This prayer has been prayed about healing: "Lord, heal this one that is sick, *if it be Thy will*." It has been prayed about financial needs and about the salvation of a loved one. Thinking that something may not be His will, people have prayed, "If it be Thy will," but let's see the reality behind the words in this chapter and the things that really were happening.

Gethsemane means "winepress." Jesus never went anywhere unless He knew where He was going. So His visit to this particular garden was not by chance. The first Chaldean root word is *gath*. That is a vat used in the treading down of the grapes to bring out the juice. The second root word, *shemen*, means any form of liquid. It is also used in certain verses of the Old Testament for the *anointing*. From this term, the English word *semen*, the substance of reproduction, is derived. What we see in this word, then, is that a grape is put in a vat and pressed until the unhindered flow of the pure juice comes forth.

Keep thy *heart* with all diligence; for out of it are the issues of life (Prov. 4:23). The issuing forth of life is from the heart.

We know that our bodies are the temple of the Holy Spirit. As a result of knowing that we are spirit, soul, and body, we can correlate the components of a Christian to the tabernacle where the Shekinah glory of God was in the Holy of Holies. It is the *shemen*, the anointing, that has the power to bring change to a life.

We are the **habitation of God through the Spirit** (Eph. 2:22), and the true forces of life are locked up in the spirit man. God is beginning a work to bring it forth. It is a work of brokenness — the breaking of the outer for the release of the inner. (We will deal more with this subject in the chapters "The Release of the Spirit" and "Beauty in Brokenness.") There is a brokenness that God wants to come to our lives. There has been very wrong teaching in this area, but by the Word of God, we can begin to see the reality. The purpose of brokenness is for the release of the precious issues from the spirit man.

Another area of confusion in the Body is going to be cleared up through a true understanding of what happened to Jesus in the Garden of Gethsemane in the area of suffering. We need to know in what we are to fellowship in the area of His suffering and what death He died to which we are to be made conformable. **That I may know Him, and the power of His resurrection,** and the fellowship of his sufferings, being made conformable unto his death (Phil. 3:10).

Soul Under Pressure

Gethsemane was a place of pressure for the purpose of bringing forth the issues of life from Jesus. The forces of life were in His spirit, not in His soul or body. Christ wanted to break forth over the whole world to bring forth life or reproduction after His kind.

And he began to be *sorrowful* **and** *very heavy.* **Then saith he unto them, My soul** *(psuche)* **is** *exceeding sorrowful,* **even unto death: tarry ye here, and watch with me** (Matt. 26:37,38). He began to be very distressed as pressure began to come upon His soul. Luke recorded it this way:

> And being in an agony he prayed more earnestly: and his sweat was as it were great drops of blood falling down to the ground.
>
> **Luke 22:44**

Why was His sweat as **drops of blood?** In the Book of Leviticus, we are told that the life of the flesh is in the blood. The word translated *life* in Leviticus is *nephesh* or "soul," the Old Testament counterpart to *psuche* in the New Testament. We are able to see that the self-life of Christ and His blood are synonymous in terminology. He poured out His soul unto death. Isaiah 53 says that He poured out His self-life. Jesus knew in the garden that He was about to lose the self-life in its totality.

Not one time do we ever find Jesus challenging the life and will of His Father for His self-life. For over 33 years, there was *never* a distinction between the will of Jesus and the will of the Father, because they were one.

I can of mine own self do nothing: as I hear, I judge: and my judgment is just; because I seek not mine own will, but the will of the Father which hath sent me (John 5:30).

Jesus had a will of His own, but He was totally submitted to the will of the Father. Yet, here in Gethsemane, for the first time in the Scriptures, we find a clear distinction, a *merismos*, between His will and the will of the Father. In fact, "letting the cup pass from Him" was His own will coming from His soul. Jesus was in a position at that moment to operate by His *psuche*, not from His *zoe*. How could that be?

Man's personality and lifestyle are in the soulish realm, and when the soul will rise up the most is when you come face to face with death — your death. The reality that Jesus was about to literally die brought out the number one area of the soul — self-preservation. The strongest force of man in the earth today is self-preservation with its ramifications of defenses, excuses, and all the other protective mechanisms.

Jesus was facing an extinction of *psuche*, a complete and total absorption into God through death, burial, and resurrection, where self no longer exists as an independent individual. Jesus had come face to face with the only way of fulfilling a total uniting with the Father — that they may be one, even as we are one (John 17:22).

The only way you will do that is when you finally come to the end of yourself. Jesus, by the power of His Spirit, absorbs you into Himself. Then your life is hidden with Christ in God. You are in the world but no longer of it. You walk and speak as He did and with His words. He was so absorbed into His Father that He could say, **He that hath seen me hath seen the**

Father (John 14:9). You no longer represent yourself, but Him. You don't substitute your own will, but represent God's will. Jesus did it, and you can come to the place where you can, also.

Three things Jesus did that revealed how much He was one with His Father:

> For I came down from Heaven, not to do mine own will, but the *will* of him that sent me.
>
> John 6:38

> Believest thou not that I am in the Father, and the Father in me? the *words* that I speak unto you I speak not of myself: but the Father that dwelleth in me, he doeth the *works*.
>
> John 14:10

The *will,* the *work,* and the *Word* of His Father were what He fulfilled, not His own will, work, or word. There was no distinction until the Garden of Gethsemane. His sweat was like great drops of blood, because the moment had come when He had to lose His *psuche.* The firstfruits of losing it were when His life began to ebb away from His pores in the form of blood. The inevitable was at hand. Personality independent of God was about to cease.

What was *the cup* of which He had to drink? The cup was that of suffering the death of self. Let us look at the Word to get the revelation of God, rather than man's opinions.

The Sacrifice of *Psuche*

Let's find out from Scripture what the deaths were that Jesus experienced. What was the price that He really paid? Look at Isaiah 53:10,11.

Yet it pleased the Lord to bruise him; he hath put him to grief: when thou shalt make his soul (*nephesh*) **an offering for sin** (What became the offering for sin? Was it His spirit, soul, or body? The answer is His *soul*.)

He shall see his seed, he shall prolong his days, and the pleasure of the Lord shall prosper in his hand. He (God, the Father) **shall see of the travail of his soul, and shall be satisfied:** (When did God see the travail of His *psuche*? God saw His travail in the Garden of Gethsemane. When God saw it, He was satisfied because the Lamb of God was bearing the offering for sin in His soul. He was made sin for our souls and was offering up His body as a living sacrifice that He might die unto Himself and that we might have life (*zoe*) in abundance. He did not have to die in His spirit to accomplish that.)

By his knowledge shall my righteous servant justify many; for he shall bear their iniquities. What was this Man's knowledge that justified me? What did He know that no one else knew? He knew the *merismos*. He knew how to get His soul under control. How do you bring control to the soul? **In your patience possess ye your souls** (Luke 21:19). Patience is *hupomone,* which means "consistency."

Watch the consistency of Jesus as we look at Isaiah 53:12. **Therefore will I** *divide him* **a portion with the great.** Did God divide Him at Gethsemane? Did a *merismos* take place before He went to the cross? The cross was the *product* of Gethsemane, the direct result of surrender. Jesus Himself died on Calvary, but He died *to Himself* in Gethsemane. The result of Gethsemane was the accomplishment at Calvary:

And he shall divide the spoil with the strong; because he hath poured out his soul *unto*

death: **and he was numbered with the transgressors; and he bare the sin of many, and
made intercession for the transgressors.**

Isaiah 53:12

In John 12, we find the prophetic utterance of Jesus
concerning Himself.

**Verily, verily, I say unto you, Except a corn
of wheat fall into the ground and die, it
abideth alone:** (notice the knowledge He had
that justified many) **but if it die, it bringeth
forth much fruit.**

He that loveth his life *(psuche)* **shall lose it;
and he that hateth his life** *(psuche)* **in this
world shall keep it unto life** *(zoe)* **eternal.**

**If any man serve me, let him follow me; and
where I am, there shall also my servant be:
if any man serve me, him will my Father
honor.**

John 12:24-26

He means that when your life *(psuche)* comes to
an end, wherever He is, there is where you will be, but
as long as you *(psuche)* are alive, wherever He goes, you
may not want to go. So, wherever He is, you may not
be. He is saying that if a man will "fall into the ground
and die," he will bring forth much fruit, "and if he loses
his life absorbed into Mine, We will give him My life,
which is life eternal, and as My servant, wherever I am,
there shall he be."

They that are led by the Spirit are the *huios,* the
fully matured sons of God. You can be born again and
not follow Him. You are going to have to grow up to
understand what it is to be led by the Spirit. The reason
we are not absorbed and have not become one with

Him is because we still love our lives. We have too much self-love and self-adoration. We are just too good to die!

We need to understand that the world really is not waiting for you and me as we have been. We have been just like the world. The Church has enough pulpit personality, expertise, and polished rhetoric to bring a congregation into the apex of soulish reaction. Christians say, "I would see Jesus; I would see Jesus," but because Christians love, protect, cherish, preserve, guard, and keep their lives so much, they do not see Jesus. As a result, the forces of life are not brought forth. Instead, displays of self-interest and self-motivation are brought forth.

Rather than bringing Christ to the forefront, most Christians want to use whatever they can as a springboard for their own glory. Many of them love themselves so much they have moved into idolatry, or self-adoration and self-worship. We are nothing without Christ. Jesus, Himself, said, **I can of mine own self do nothing** (John 5:30). Paul, too, realized this truth, but he also said, **I can do all things through Christ which strengtheneth me** (Phil. 4:13).

All the religiosity that tries to build up self, and all the positives that exalt self as God, stink! All you are going for when you follow that line is what Satan offered Adam and Eve in the very beginning, **Ye shall be as gods** (Gen. 3:5).

The difference between what Satan offers as god and what God offers is that *Deity came down to humanity to serve*, but man wants to lift himself up to be a lord and ruler over himself and others — **I *will* ascend into heaven . . . I *will* be like the most high** (Isa. 14:13,14). We must come down before we can go up. The soul must come down so that the spirit can go up.

Jesus was prophesying that He could fall into the ground and personality, independent of God, could come to an end. **Yea, though we have known Christ after the flesh, yet now henceforth know we him no more** (2 Cor. 5:16b). Some people still see me as Randy Shankle, after the flesh, but I am learning that I am a son of God who is being absorbed into Him. I have been to the Mount of Transfiguration.

We can now see that the terms *soul, life,* and *psuche* are synonymous. It is important that you understand that Jesus laid down His *psuche* life, because Gethsemane is a lifestyle. Every time my soul begins to rise up, the call of my spirit takes me to Gethsemane. There the squeeze is on to remove all the garbage in order for God to bring forth the true anointing. It is the breaking of the outer shell to get into the inner man.

Christ Lays Down His *Psuche*

Jesus said in John 10, "I have the power to give My life or to preserve My life. I have that authority. No man is going to take My life, but I am going to choose one day to lay it down that you may have zoe and have it more abundantly. I am going to lay down My life that I may bring forth the power of reproduction, the true spiritual 'semen' of God, so there can be a reproduction after His kind of new creatures all over the earth."

The thief cometh not, but for to steal, and to kill, and to destroy: I am come that they might have life (*zoe,* the God-life), and that they might have it more abundantly.

I am the good shepherd: the good shepherd giveth his life (psuche) for the sheep.

124

> Therefore doth my Father love me, because
> I lay down my life (psuche), that I might take
> it again.
>
> No man taketh it from me, but I lay it down
> of myself. I have power to lay it down, and
> I have power to take it again. This command-
> ment have I received of my Father.
>
> John 10:10,11,17,18

Now, go back to Gethsemane. Understand that this is going to happen in your life, time and time again. If you do not understand it when it begins to take place, you will resist the purpose of God and never come out of it right. You will blow it every time.

Then saith He unto them, my soul is exceeding sorrowful, even unto death (Matt. 26:38). Have we established clearly that it was His soul, or self-life, that He was going to pour out? He poured out His blood, the life *(nephesh)* of the flesh. God said that upon whatever doorpost the blood was sprinkled, the angel of death would pass over. (Ex. 12:13.) Can he see your blood? He cannot, if it hasn't been poured out, nor if it is still retained within the vessel that is you.

Just as the alabaster box was broken to release the precious fragrance and perfume (Matt. 26:7), so the outer man must be broken in order for the true anointing and fragrance of God to pour forth. Often, however, people don't want that. They do not want to be dealt with and broken by God, and when the curse comes, it will not pass over you. You cannot reverse the curse. There is no blood on the doorposts. God told every Israelite and family to do it. As long as you continue to preserve your life *(psuche)*, you will not be able to minister life *(zoe)* effectively to others.

We all begin the Christian life absorbed within ourselves, but the only way we are *supposed* to be is as the Son of Man: **For even the Son of man came not to be ministered unto, but to minister, and to give his life** *(psuche)* **a ransom for many** (Mark 10:45). Live as He did, not to be ministered unto, but to minister, to pour out. The entire revelation of Communion is of broken bread and poured-out wine. You cannot distribute it until you break it and pour it out.

> **And as they were eating, Jesus took bread, and blessed it, and** *brake it,* **and gave it to the disciples, and said, take, eat; this is my body.**
>
> **And he took the cup, and gave thanks, and gave it to them, saying, drink ye** *all* **of it.**
>
> **For this is my blood of the new testament** (covenant)**, which is shed for many for the remission of sins.**
>
> **Matthew 26:26-28**

In taking Communion, we are drinking of the life that Jesus poured out. We are identifying with the revelation that as we drink, our lives have ceased. We are no longer our own. We have become broken bread and poured-out wine, broken and distributed to others to take to them the *zoe* of God.

Was it possible for the cup to pass from Jesus? Was it possible for Him to be delivered from the situation? Yes. Remember when Peter tried to save Jesus from the soldiers? Jesus said He could have called for legions of angels at that moment. A way out is what most people look for when God wants to lead them to Gethsemane. I am not talking about financial pressures or pressures of sickness. I am talking about the pressure that comes

126

on the soul for only one reason — to break the strength of the soul in order for the spirit to be strengthened. **Nevertheless, not as I will but as thou wilt** (v.39). Not the will of my soul, but the will of my Father — a clear distinction between two wills.

When Jesus first returned to the disciples and found them asleep, how long had He been in travail and heaviness? *One hour.* He told them to watch and pray, reminding them that the **spirit indeed is willing, but the flesh is weak. He went away the** *second time,* **and prayed, saying, O my Father, if this cup may not pass away from me, except I drink it, thy will be done** (vs.41,42).

The first time, His soul had cried out, "There has got to be a way out. How about a legion of angels?" He caught Himself, however, and submitted to the Father's will. It took him an hour to get that far. He went right back in for another hour, and now we begin to see a surrendering of the soul to the will of the Father. We begin to see the soul submitted willing and obedient to the spirit. The soul is being dealt with. Jesus, the *Merismos* Man, is winning over His soul. If He had not, there would have been no Redeemer. If He had not fallen as a seed into the ground, He would have remained alone, just as millions of others remain alone who do nothing for anyone else.

Then He returned a second time and found the disciples asleep. He left them to go away and pray **the third time, saying the same words** (v.44). It took the Master of the *merismos* three hours of prayer to bring His soul under control to where it would willingly relinquish its position and life, but there was a hope that anchored His soul. That hope was you and me. Because of that expectation, He dropped anchor in Gethsemane, and said:

"No, Soul, you are not going to get your way. You are not going to do what you want to do. You are going to stay here under the pressure of God until you submit, even if it takes all night long. You are going to come out of here willing and ready. I am ready to do what my Father told me to do."

Jesus laid down His psuche so that you and I can have zoe!

"Watch and Pray"

Gethsemane is a place of pressure for the purpose of breaking the strengths of the soul. The soul will not want to go there and, certainly, will not want to stay, but you need to take him and keep him there until it is finished. The revelation of how to handle Gethsemane is found in Matthew 26:41: **Watch and pray, that ye enter not into temptation.**

I have learned that those two powerful words, *watch* and *pray,* are what keep me from choosing my own life and future destiny. If my *psuche* rises up, then my spirit rises up also and says, "To Gethsemane with you!" My soul stands before God until he submits. When God sees the blood, He will pass over. He will pardon, once the life is poured out.

There are two ways to get into temptation: You *enter* or you *fall.* Matthew 26:41 says, **Watch and pray, that ye *enter* not into temptation,** and James 1:2 says, **Count it all joy when ye *fall* into divers temptations.** The temptations you *fall* into, you are to count as joy because God has made a way out. However, when you *enter,* you do it with knowledge. You cannot enter a door unless you know it is there. Falling, on the other hand, is the result of not knowing a snare was there. The devil set something up, and you fell into it. However you get into temptation, God can get you out of it by providing a way out when you fall or by deliverance when you knowingly enter in and then repent.

The interesting thing is that when you *enter* into temptation by wrong reasoning, by wrong thought processes (as we saw in the previous chapter), it costs you something. It is a tough way to go, even though God will bail you out. It takes a long time to recapture where you were and to recover the ground lost by the mistake. I have known people who, under a time of pressure, begin to do irrational things. They wanted to harm something or tear up their pickup truck or beat something.

Under a time of pressure, and that is what Gethsemane was, the soul wanted out of the whole thing, while the spirit man wanted the will of God. Jesus said that, during this time of pressure when it does not look as if anything is going on, when it does not seem as if God is speaking, and things seem to be falling apart, we *watch and pray*. What are we to watch? We are to watch over the soul man. That is the time to take heed and take a close look at your soul man, because he is about to come alive if you don't watch it.

In a place of pressure, there is no comfort for the soul. It is comfort he is looking for, but comfort he will not get because it is not a time of comfort. It is a time of trust. Faith is the force you have to use in times of pressure. Set a watchman around the soul man and put the Word of God as a hedge around him. Anything that comes through the soul independent of the teaching and training of the Word, I will not activate or enter into. I have learned to watch for anything that would initiate a release valve to bring comfort to the soul during these times. Understand, now, that I am

129

not talking about a martyr complex, but in times of pressure, the soul does not need comfort or rest. It needs to be calmed down or quieted.

He wants to be comforted, to be patted on the back and told everything is okay. Psalm 131:2 talks about the soul, or the self, being calmed and quieted like a child who has been weaned from the milk and drawn from the breast. The child gets fretful, irritable, and frustrated because he wants milk, and if he isn't weaned, he is going to win over you. He needs to be calmed, settled down, and under control, not catered to with a pacifier, or comforted.

Set a watchman over your soul, and every time he wants to start something or get involved in something that would bring him comfort, deny him. He doesn't have to be constantly told, "Everything is okay." If you are in the hands of God, the soul should *know* that everything is okay. Comforting him simply reinforces the fears and anxieties. Your soul needs to know that God just has you on hold for a while, and that He will come and rain righteousness on you, then the fruit will come forth. It will be obvious.

During this process, wait for the clouds, wait for the thunder and lightning, and wait for them to do their job. At this time, set a watchman, your spirit, over your soul and gird up the loins of your mind. Tighten your thought processes so they will not run rampant.

Gethsemane: a Place of Pressure

By telling them to **watch and pray,** Jesus was telling the disciples how *not* to enter into temptation. What was the temptation Jesus was facing? He was facing the choice to save His own life. That was the exact thing all eleven disciples also were about to face. So He told them, "If you will watch and pray, you will not enter."

**Who his own self bare our sins in his own
body on the tree, that we, being dead to sins,
should live unto righteousness: by whose
stripes ye were healed.**

**For ye were as sheep going stray; but are now
returned unto the Shepherd and Bishop of
your souls.**

1 Peter 2:24,25

Pastors have a two-fold job: *poimen*, shepherd, and
episkope, bishop. Jesus is the true Shepherd and Bishop,
or Overseer of the soul. He was the Shepherd and
Bishop over His own soul, as well. Watch what? Pray
to whom? What does a watchman do? Jesus' spirit man's
authority was watching over His soul, because if He
didn't, the soul was about to "*psuche* out." His spirit
would not permit it and would take Him back into
prayer however many times it took and regardless of
what future events the soul thought he was ready to
handle.

Is Gethsemane a one-time experience like the new
birth? No! **Receive with meekness the engrafted word,
which is able to save your souls** (James 1:21b). Get him
saved in the mind, by transformation; get him saved
in the will, by willingly falling upon the Rock; and, get
your senses exercised with spiritual oversight.

**Feed the flock of God which is among you, taking
the oversight** (*episkopeo*) (1 Pet. 5:2a). Are you supposed
to *take* oversight, or *wait* for it? Take it, or you'll never
have it. **Remember them which have the rule over you
. . .** (Heb. 13:7). There are people who are to rule over
your *psuche.* **Obey them that have the rule over you,
and submit yourselves: for they watch for your souls,
as they that must give account, that they may do it with**

joy, and not with grief: for that is unprofitable for you (Heb. 13:17).

People do not like the true bishop ministry that deals with soulish displays. Most Christians do not want to submit to anyone who will talk to them about their souls, because they do not want to lose their independent lifestyle, but it is simply *rebellion* not to submit. Why? We are under the commandment of Almighty God to submit to the authority of the Word.

The *watching* of Matthew 26:41 is to watch over your soul. The purpose of *praying* is to strengthen your spirit, enabling it to rise up in oversight of the soul.

If Jesus had not won at Gethsemane, He would never have made it to Calvary, but when they hung Him on the cross and the blood came forth, it justified many. You must believe it to receive it, and you must apply it in your life.

Gethsemane is a place of pressure. The pressure that came on Jesus was to seek and save His life, but because of His knowledge of the *merismos* (the dividing asunder of soul and spirit), He justified many, and knew how to bring control to His soul, how to anchor it, and how to allow God to work brokenness into it. Christ, the grape, dropped into Gethsemane, the wine vat, and the pressure of the Father came upon His soul. The Spirit of God would not let Him go until the true anointing came forth. It squeezed upon Jesus until He became sorrowful and very heavy, even unto death. When He did, the new wine, the juice of the grape, came forth to intoxicate the world with His aroma and taste, and the fragrance filled the earth. Even now, it continues to draw men to Christ. They will drink of Him until they cannot live without His influence.

Sin does not make you selfish. Selfishness makes you sin. It causes you to be drawn away of your own lusts and enticed. After *merismos*, you live not as the *psuchikos* (soulish) man, but as the *pneumatikos* (spiritual) man. Every time the soul tries to exert his position, you need to take him off to Gethsemane until the true anointing comes forth again and he stops *"psuche-ing"* out.

10

UNDERSTANDING THE *PSUCHE* REALM

We have looked at the areas of soulish activity and have learned how the soul gets saved progressively, as opposed to the instantaneous salvation of the spirit. Now I want to deal with the understanding of the soulish realm. That realm needs a lot of understanding!

Psuche is the seat of personality, but your soul is not the real you. The real you is your spirit man. As a result, your spirit man emanates or transmits the real life of God, or the real, real you. There is another aspect of you, however, called the soul man that makes up your personality — the *seat* of personality — the way you are in temperament and characteristics and traits, which is the way you think, operate, etc.

To a major degree, people have not understood this. They are saying, "Who am I? What is my soul man? How does he operate? What about my temperament? What about my personality? What about my characteristics?" Let's bring some understanding in this area because the soul man is seen very clearly in the scriptures in a very, very beautiful definition.

We are triune: spirit, soul, and body. When God gave us authority in the Book of Genesis, He gave us dominion and, in this dominion, He gave us the power and the authority to have control and influence in the earth today. In doing so, He made us triune — spirit, soul, and body. The aspect, or part of man, in whom

God placed the authority was the spirit. It is through the spirit of man that we are to rule and have dominion and control. The spirit man has dominion over the animals because animals are dualistic, just body and soul. Therefore, we can control their thoughts, their wills, their choices, or their emotions. This control is called *dominion*.

Dominion Over the Soul

An animal does not do what he wants to do every time. He will live where you live, sleep where you make him a place, and eat what you feed him. He is very much in subjection to you. In like manner, the spirit people in the earth today are to rule and have dominion over our souls. Our soul man never was intended by God to have dominion or to rule and reign in life. He was supposed to be subservient to the spirit man. Your spirit is supposed to rule over your soul. The dominating, controlling force is to come through the spirit, not the soul.

People have tried to counterfeit that through the use of soulish or psychic powers, intimidation, exploitation, or manipulation by means of soul power. They use a loud voice, or some type of body control, or their personality to rule or to take dominion and control. That is not the way of God. That is the way of man. We are coming to understand the soulish realm and to realize that the real person is the spirit.

The soul was not supposed to move independently of the spirit but to wait until the spirit initiated action, then respond. The soul man now reacts or responds *before* the spirit man most of the time, and that is out of order. It is the spirit that receives the revealed will of God and, once it does, the soul is to be the doer of that will. **But as the servants of Christ, doing the will of God from the heart** (*psuche*) (Eph. 6:6). The soul man is to do the will of God after he hears the spirit man speak and give him instruction and direction. It is then that we are able to do what God has told us to do.

> **Then said Jesus unto his disciples, If any man will come after me, let him deny himself, and take up his cross, and follow me.**
>
> **For whosoever will save his life** (*psuche*) **shall lose it: and whosoever will lose his life** (*psuche*) **for my sake shall find it.**
>
> **For what is a man profited, if he shall gain the whole world, and lose his own soul** (*psuche*)**? or what shall a man give in exchange for his soul** (*psuche*)**?**
>
> Matthew 16:24-26

The King James Version uses both *life* and *soul* to translate *psuche.* Well, that is fine, because the life of the soul is the life of the man — the self-ruled life or the self-man. If you deal with the word *soul*, you deal with yourself. If you deal with the word *self* or *life* or *soul*, you deal with your own life, your own self, the self-life, or the soul-life. They are synonymous terms that denote your life independent of God's life, *zoe.*

When you were born again, you got the *zoe* of God, or the life of God, but you also have the life of self or your self-life. In understanding the soulish realm, God's Word teaches us what to do. We are to deny ourselves. Now that has brought the Church into a wrong teaching, because there is a difference between denial of self and self-denial.

Deny Self or Self-Denial?

Matthew 16:24 says, **. . . if any man will come after me, let him deny himself.** Notice that it does not say "self-denial," but "deny himself." What does this mean? Does this mean denying yourself the right to drink coffee or sleep or to call a fast and deny yourself food so that you can have your soul dealt with or saved? No! What the Word is saying is, **Deny your*self*.** The man who would follow Jesus must **deny *himself*.** That means he must deny his soul the right to live, to move, or to choose independently of God.

When the soul says, "Do you know what I am going to do today?" you deny him that choice because the Word of God does not give him that privilege. He does not have the right to do what he wants to do, go where he wants to go, live where he wants to live, or all the other things in a self-made lifestyle. He does not have that right.

Paul said, . . . **I die daily** (1 Cor. 15:31). He simply meant, "I realize that in Christ I now live and move and have my being. I will die daily. I deny myself, my mind, my will, and my emotions the right to move independently of God." To find the life of God, I must deny my own self, and in so doing (as Matthew 16:25 says), in losing my life, I will save it.

If you were to gain the whole world and lose your own soul, what would you have gained? Nothing! You can have everything and your soul be unsaved, yet gain nothing in life. Luke 9:23,24 says:

> **And he said to them all, if any man will come after me, let him deny himself, and take up his cross daily, and follow me.**

> **For whosoever will save his life shall lose it: but whosoever will lose his life for my sake, the same shall save it.**

When did Jesus say to take up the cross and follow Him? He said to take up your cross daily. Now we have missed the truth in these verses through religion. Religious tradition says that the cross represents some form of suffering or sickness. "I have to put up with this" or "Paul had his cross to bear" or "The thorn in the flesh or sickness can be a cross." No! No! That is not what the Word says. Sickness and disease are not crosses. Being in poverty or beaten down and defeated are not crosses in life that God wants you to bear. It is "religion" that teaches that trash, not God's Word.

The Word says this: You must deny your*self*, take up *your* cross. Tell me, what is the cross? What was the cross of Jesus Christ? The cross of Jesus was the death of Christ Himself. He died on Calvary on the cross, so the cross does not represent sickness and disease. It represents death to your *self*. You must deny yourself the right to live independently of God and recognize that you must die daily.

Every day I pick up the cross of the Christ-life and say, "Thank God, I identify with the cross and that I am crucified with Christ. I am dead. My self-life, my selfish life, living my own way, doing what I want to do, is dead. That stuff does not exist anymore. I no longer can do that. Thank God for it." That is picking up your cross daily. That is the cross you choose.

The number one step in dealing with the soul man is to *deny him*. You deny him the right and privilege of everything. Don't give him the opportunity to try to figure things out, to rationalize things, to get into reasoning and logic and come up with all his ridiculous conclusions of what is happening. *When God is not speaking, you don't know what is happening.* You just know Who is doing it, and that is all you need to know. The soul always wants to have some reasoning or some understanding of what is happening.

"Why is this happening? What is going on right now? What is taking place? My goodness, I can't figure this thing out!" No, you can't figure it out, and God is not going to do it for you. It is not a time of reasoning, it is a time of faith and trust. If you do not know how to trust God, the soul will want to be comforted and will insist on knowing what is happening. In the times of pressure, the place of Gethsemane, God will not comfort or pacify your soul, but another source will be glad to tell you "what is happening." You'll be comforted with "knowledge," but you're going to come up wrong. You'll say, "Oh, now I see what is happening." No, you don't. You do not see anything until God speaks.

You can ask me, "Why does God have us wait until He rains righteousness?" (Hos. 10:12.) I don't know. I just know that we are to wait because God says to wait. I may have some understanding of some of the end results, but I don't know all the "ins and outs" of it. I know He is going to bring rain, which is going to bring a new anointing. I know that, but it doesn't comfort me during those times. I'm like a starving plant that is prophesied to: "I'll bring you rain in six months." Hey, what about now?

I always enjoy the rain of God's anointing and presence and power and purpose, but when it is not there, I have to understand something called *trust*. Until you understand God's authority, your reasoning will miss Him because *it is the love of God and the fear of His authority that make reasonings bow.* Reason will challenge the authority of God's Word, if you have no fear or respect or understanding of the authority of God and His Word or of God through man.

Your reasoning faculty will rise up and challenge the Word. That is called, **. . . every high thing that**

exalteth itself against the knowledge of God . . .
(2 Cor. 10:5) against the knowledge of His Word. If you
don't think that is pride, you are wrong. It is pride in
a proud soulish realm that wants to exalt itself against
the Word and say, "I don't care what the Word says,
I'm not waiting any longer."

You are in rebellion, and **rebellion is as the sin of
witchcraft, and stubbornness as iniquity and idolatry**
(1 Sam. 15:23). Do you see where that is coming from
and who is behind it? Obviously, that attitude is not
of God. That is why Jesus said to **watch and pray** at
this time. Put a watchman over the thought processes
and pray. Why would He admonish us to pray during
these times? He knows that prayer is the last thing the
soul wants to do then. The last place he wants to go
is on his knees to God. You say:

"It's like a stone wall. The heavens are brass. I've
walked the floor, and I've prayed. I sought God and
said, 'What do you want me to do? What is going on?' "

He didn't speak, and you don't want to pray. You
are tired of praying because it seems not to be working anyway. You are about to "*psuche* out." When you
get into that frame of mind, you are about to move over
into the demonic realm. You have just entered a hornet's
nest, and you are going to be deceived and come out
of this thing stung.

I have made a commitment as the years have gone
by. I have gained on this thing. I have received more
revelation and have told God I would be faithful to
deliver to the Body of Christ the things He has taught
me in the Word during these dry spells. The reason
rain comes is because we have dry spells, is it not? That
is exactly what these times feel like, "dry spells."

You begin a meeting and lift your hands to say, "All right, Father, thank You for your presence," and there is no presence; "Thank You for Your power," and there is no power; "Thank You for Your direction," and there is no direction. It is called a "dry spell." Just move with God in what you know, and you had better know the Word. All through the years, I have learned and gained ground through the "dry spells" and have told God I would be faithful to deliver at times like those.

The Unsaved Soul Remains Childish

The Word of God teaches us the understanding of the *psuche* realm. We must understand it because the soul man does not want to be denied. The soul man is graphically represented as a child. A child does not want to be denied. If he doesn't get *his* way, he throws a temper tantrum. Children want *what they* want *when they* want it, or *they* throw a fit. That is what I call "*psuche* souffle." That is soulish. That needs to be dealt with.

Don't try to rule your children with your soul. Rule the children with your spirit by the Word of God. Many people try to rule their children by saying, "If you do that again, I'm gonna . . . ." There is no authority in that. You are not using the authority of your spirit. You are using a method of intimidation called "fear." You are provoking fear in them, and they will not fear you or respect your authority. They only fear the consequences. That is wrong training.

Don't pick up a belt or a paddle and say, "I'll whip you with this *if* . . . ." No, when you draw it, fire it. If you don't, you will teach that child to respond to circumstances, not to authority. Don't threaten children. I have seen parents who would tell a child something once, then tell him twice, then, when the child did not do anything, say, "One, two, three . . . ." I'm sure you have seen that kind of correction, but that is not the way the Word of God teaches. That is soulish correction. The child is responding to the countdown, not to authority.

We are teaching children wrongly because we do not understand the *psuche* realm. When you come to understand that realm, you will see that a child is triune — spirit, soul, and body — but that he *acts* dualistic, just soul and body. The soul is the self-ruled, self-governed lifestyle. He wants what he wants when he wants it. If he does not get it, he is going to see to it that everybody around is miserable. That child needs correction to the soul. Correction comes through the spirit by the Word. The soul does not rule the spirit. If the soul ruled the spirit, then animals could have dominion over humans.

I have some Arabian horses, and I like to work with them. Because I understand the *merismos* teaching and the *psuche* realm, I know that a horse is mind, will, emotions, and a physical body. Therefore, when I begin training a horse, I don't break him. That is what cowboys do — *psuche* training or breaking the *psuche*. The macho cowboy says, "I'll break his spirit." In other words, force versus force. The ego of the cowboy is going to rule over the horse so he can say, "See, I won." That is *psuche*.

You shouldn't try to "break" a horse, but "train" a horse. The soul realm does not need to be broken. It needs to be trained. That is how you do it. You take the mind, will, and emotions of an animal, or of a child before that child is born again, and deal with them through the authority of your spirit. Even regenerate people may not be controlled by their spirits. Some are even ruled by demonic spirits through their souls (called "super-soul"). That, however, is a different situation than training a child or a horse, which is simply dealing with a basic soul problem.

What do you do with an animal? What do you do with a child? What do you do with an unregenerate person? You must deal with them through the means of their soul. Your child's temper tantrums are based on selfishness. Sin was dealt with 2,000 years ago. Self is not yet dealt with. Jesus forgave us of our sin and washed that away, but we still have a "self" problem.

When I am riding my horse and he goes to the right, but I want him to go to the left, I have reins. What are reins for? They are to control the soul, or the will, of the horse and to turn him the way I want him to go. So it is with a child, although the "reins" are invisible authority. I have heard parents say, "I'll get it for you later," when they were being evasive about a child's request, trying to put him off so he would forget. Don't play games with the child. If he should not have or do something, tell him, "No." You are dealing with his soul. What do you do with the soul? You deny it.

For example, a minister friend of mine had a young boy who was afraid to be away from mama and daddy all the time. He was too old for that type of reaction, but he was afraid of everything. They had never dealt with his soul or weaned his soul. One day, they came out to visit me where I was working with my horses. A little puppy ran out of the house, and the boy began to panic and scream, "Daddy, Daddy."

His father reached down, picked him up, and said, "It's okay. It's okay."

I said, "Brother, you need to set your son down because you just reinforced his fears. There is nothing to fear."

The adult is the one who should be able to determine if there really is something to fear. If so, then take the child to safety. Parents are the "overseers" or the "bishops" of the child's soul. If there is anything to be afraid of, such as a rattlesnake, then take the child out of the way and bring security to his soul *and* body. If it's only a puppy, don't pick the child up and reinforce the fear. A little puppy is no valid reason for fear.

By kneeling down and petting the puppy and saying, "It's all right. The puppy is not going to hurt you," you are reinforcing areas of the soul. Remember, the soul is the selfish lifestyle, or your personality. All children are very *psuche* unless they are dealt with. Leave a child to himself, and he will get more and more selfish. You must learn as a spiritual parent how to deal with his soul through your spirit. The same thing is happening with God. God is dealing with our soulish realm through our spirits. Our spirits must take dominion over our souls.

Weaning of the Soul

The soulish aspect of man is like a child. If he doesn't get what he wants or get his way, he becomes fretful, irritable, angry, and throws a temper tantrum or sulks and pouts. Do you know what parents usually do? They give in to that child. That is not what they are supposed to be doing. They are not to give in to that child at all. They are to deny that child. Deny your soul.

Whom shall he teach knowledge? and whom shall he make to understand doctrine? them

that are *weaned from the milk*, and drawn from the breasts.

For precept must be upon precept, precept upon precept; line upon line, line upon line; here a little, and there a little.

Isaiah 28:9,10

These scriptures are talking about the knowledge of man, understanding doctrine, and understanding the things of the spirit. Isaiah makes it very clear in these verses just who God is going to teach knowledge to and who is going to have understanding of doctrine. Who is this guy? He is the one who has been weaned from the milk.

If you get up in the morning and your soul says, "I'm going to go buy that" or "I'm going to do this," your spirit should rise up as the overseer and say, "No, you won't do anything until you check in with me because I deny you the right to move independently of God."

"But I want to do it!"

"I'm sorry. I am going to wean you right now. You are as a rebellious, fretting child, and I am going to start the weaning process."

Go to Psalm 131:1,2:

Lord, my heart is not haughty, nor mine eyes lofty: neither do I exercise myself in great matters, or in things too high for me.

Surely I have behaved and quieted myself, *as a child that is weaned of his mother: my soul is even as a weaned child.*

The *Amplified Bible* says, *Surely I have calmed and quieted my soul* (v.2). In calming and quieting your soul, you are dealing with a child. The writer of the Psalm was saying his soul was even as a weaned child . . . **I have behaved and quieted my soul.** What is he really saying here? He is saying you are not going to come to understand knowledge and be taught doctrine or understand the ways of God until your soul gets weaned.

When the Word of God says, **By his stripes you were healed,** *psuche* will say, "Well, I just don't believe that." Your soul needs to be weaned of that right then. You have to deal directly with the Word of God in relationship to submission of your soul. James 4:7 says, **Submit yourselves therefore to God. Resist the devil, and he will flee from you.** To whom is he talking? He is talking to the soul man. Submit to God, resist the devil, and he will flee from you. What we want to do most of the time is submit to the devil and resist God! In that case, God will flee from us also. We do not want to submit to God, but we don't want the devil to mess with us either.

The order is: submit to God, then resistance will be effective. To submit to God is to submit to His Word. Do you see that? When you submit to His Word, you are submitting to God. When you do that, the devil flees from you. The soul man wants his own way. He does not want to be dealt with or denied. He does not want to be weaned. He wants what he wants when he wants it.

Husband, you are the head over your household. Get up and go to church. Pay your tithes. Whether you want to or not, do it. It is the Word of God. Submit to that. Get involved in the Kingdom of God. Be about your Father's business, and your Father will be about your business. If you don't like the way your business is being run, it is probably because you are not running God's business so well.

The child must be weaned. When we start taking a child off milk, what happens? He begins to be fretful, irritable, and perhaps throws temper tantrums. He doesn't want to be taken off the bottle. He just lies there and cries, "I like the milk, I want the milk," until somebody stuffs the bottle in his mouth and feeds him.

That is why Christians don't want to get off the milk of the Word. They want to just lie there and be fed. They want to go to seminars and crusades and be irresponsible. Do you know why you like to go to seminars and crusades and teaching centers? Those ministers are not pastors, they are teachers or prophets. In other words, they will teach you the Word, then go home. Most Christians like that because there is no commitment and no responsibility. They do not have to be faithful or reliable or dependable.

Christians cry, "Just give me the milk. Give me the Word. Stuff a bottle in my mouth for an hour and a half. Feed me. Feed me." When they go home and Jesus wants them to do something, they say, "I don't want to do that today."

Do you know what is happening? They are like children who need to be weaned. The other aspect is that when God begins to wean you or draw you from the milk to bring you the meat of the Word, you get irritable. Let me show you how it works through the scripture that says, **By whose stripes you were healed** (1 Pet. 2:24). You wake up tomorrow morning and feel sick. Your soul says, "I've tried this stuff. I thought it was supposed to work." *The fretting and the anxiety of the soul is like a child.*

Do you see what is happening? Your soul man is ruling your life. He should be weaned right then from that unbelief and distrust of God and fear of God's integrity. The soul should get quiet and behave quietly and calmly.

I am grateful to Jesus Christ that He has weaned me from the milk of the Word. Now, when the Word of God says I am healed, I am healed! When the Word of God says I'm prosperous, I am prosperous! When the Word says I have been delivered from the powers of darkness, I have been delivered, whether I feel like it or not. I finally got weaned from all my fretting and murmuring and complaining about why God doesn't do what He says He will do or why the Word is not true or why it wouldn't work for me and why it worked for others.

That attitude was childish. A child will cry, "Well, so-and-so got that. If so-and-so got it, I should get it. The little guy down the street got a bicycle. I should get a bicycle. Why didn't I get a bicycle?" That is so *psuche.* All that deals with is your own frustrations and irritations based on your own immaturities. We have to get the soul weaned from its fretting and anxiety.

Let me give you another example. The Word says, **But my God shall supply all your need according to his riches in glory by Christ Jesus** (Phil. 4:19). When your soul is weaned from the fretting, it won't walk the floor and say, "Oh, what are we going to do? The bills are due. How are we going to pay them?" That is all *"psuche* souffle," soulish reaction, fears, worries, and anxiety, like a child who has a problem with distrust of his parents.

When God's word says He will meet all of your need, do you know what you ought to do? You ought

148

to pull out the pacifier and throw it away, lay back in bed, and say:

"Thank God! Hallelujah! My God has met all of my needs. I don't care what the bills say. I don't care when they are due. I don't care what the telephone people have said, or what the bill collectors are going to repossess. I am not going to worry. I am not going to fret. I've rolled all of my care over on him. I've weaned my soul. I deny him the right of unbelief. I deny him the right to get me out of bed and walk the floor and pace with fear, anxiety, frustration, worry, and all the other stuff. I deny him that right."

Take the wringing of the hands and the "Oh, God, what are we going to do?" attitude, which are only pacifiers, and throw them out the window. I choose to live successfully with God. Jesus knew how to do this. He was on a boat once with the twelve disciples and a great storm was coming. Jesus was in the back of the boat sleeping while the disciples were fretting and full of fear and worry that they were going to drown. What was happening? Their souls were like children. They were full of fear and were saying, "Oh, my God, what are we going to do. We will all drown," but Jesus was in the back of the boat sleeping. Why? Right there is a revelation. His soul had been weaned from fear of dying, or of being destroyed, or of sickness, or fear of anything.

When your soul man has been dealt with by the engrafted Word that says, **By whose stripes ye were healed,** and you wake up in the morning and your neck has a big growth on it, you don't panic. When your soul has been weaned, you don't say, "Oh, my God, what happened?" Your soul says, "Oh, hallelujah, I'm healed. I was healed 2,000 years ago. I was healed yesterday,

149

so I am healed today!" The soul has been weaned from its fears.

Summary of How to Deal With the Soul

The first thing in bringing the soul into submission is to *deny* him, and the second thing is to *wean* him. Understand that your soul is like a child who wants its own way every time. That is why parents and husbands and wives get into arguments: one, or both, of them are pursuing selfish lifestyles. They want what they want when they want it. Wean that attitude in your own life. Wean it in your marital life and in your children's lives, because they are soulish.

You do this by quieting and calming the soul. You are quieting and calming him from anxiety, fear, worry, and frustration about your life. Don't you think Jesus Christ loves you? Don't you think He cares enough for you, and because He cares for you, you can roll all of your cares over on Him? When you learn this and get a firm revelation of it, you will get that bottle out of your mouth and grow up in Christ. Learn to believe, "If God says I am healed, I am healed. If God says He is going to meet my needs, He is going to meet my needs." *Then* your soul gets peaceful.

Luke 21:19 says, **In your patience possess ye your souls.** This is another area of dealing with the soul that has not been quite understood, so I want to shed some light on this aspect in the next chapter.

Scriptures for the Soul

1. *The Saving of the Soul:* Hebrews 10:39, James 1:21, 1 Peter 1:9.
2. *The Soul Preserved Blameless:* 1 Thessalonians 5:23.

3. *Prosperity (Advancing) of the Soul:* 3 John 2.
4. *Metamorphosis (transformation, a change of thinking) of the Soul:* Romans 12:2.
5. *Anchor of the Soul:* Hebrews 6:19.
6. *Weaning of the Soul:* Psalm 131:2.
7. *Fainting of the Soul:* Hebrews 12:3, Galatians 6:9, Isaiah 40:28.
8. *Control of the Soul:* Luke 21:19.
9. *Purify Your Soul:* 1 Peter 1:22. You purify your soul through obeying the Word.
10. *Shepherd and Bishop of Your Soul:* 1 Peter 2:25, Matthew 26:41.
11. *Soul to Magnify the Lord:* Luke 1:46,47.

11
CONTROLLING THE SOUL

There are two words for patience in the Greek language of the New Testament, *makrothumia* and *hupomone*. The first word denotes a form of patience that means "to put up with, to tolerate, to endure." The *King James Version* also translates it "forbearance or longsuffering or long enduring." The fruit of the Spirit, longsuffering, is translated from *makrothumia*. The second word, *hupomone*, means the "force of consistency." In Luke 21:19, **In your patience, possess ye your souls,** *patience* is *hupomone*. So Luke is saying, "In your *hupomone*, in your *consistency*, possess ye your soul."

How do you *control* the soul? Control comes through the force of patience. That is why the men of God that have preceded this teaching have taught on faith and patience. The Faith-Word movement was the cloud of God to bring us to the teaching we are receiving right now because faith is for the spirit and hope is for the soul. Here is the force of consistency: Patience brings control or possession of the soul by the spirit. When my soul is out of control, I know right then that I am not using consistency to the Word of God.

Look at James 1 where the same Greek word is used for "patience" as in Luke 21:19:

My brethren, count it all joy when ye fall into divers temptations;

Knowing this, that the trying of your faith worketh patience (*hupomone*).

152

But let patience have her perfect work, that ye may be perfect and entire, wanting nothing.

James 1:2-4

In the force of consistency, you are to be able to control the soulish realm. Remember the three things we have learned about understanding the soulish realm? The soul must be *denied* because he wants his own life; the soul must be *weaned* in order for spiritual growth to take place; and, the soul must be brought under *control*.

In doing all of this, you will bring the soul to a position where he is no longer fretting, irritable, fussy, selfish, egotistical, prideful, boastful, pushy, demanding, or controlling others. He does not just speak because he always wants to say something. I have been around people who seem to want to talk all the time. That is soulish. Get your soul under control, and you will only speak when God begins to bring you forth into utterance. I am not talking about enjoying fellowship. I am talking about giving and getting advice or opinions or views and affecting other people's lives. Don't be so talkative. Be slow to speak.

We are to count it all joy when we fall into divers temptations *knowing* this, in other words, it is something you *know*. That does not mean we are to count the trial or the test a joy, but that we are to *know* what James knew. I know that the trying of my faith works patience, or puts to work, or activates, the force of consistency. The word *worketh* does not mean to develop patience or to create it, but to activate, or to put into action, the force of consistency. God is the God of patience, *hupomone*, consistency.

He is **the same yesterday, and today, and for ever** (Heb. 13:8). God does not change. (Mal. 3:6.) When you receive the new birth in your spirit, you receive God's divine nature. In receiving God's divine nature, you are now a partaker of the force of consistency. In other words, faith and patience just work hand in hand like a husband-and-wife team. Masculine is faith and feminine is patience because "patience" is referred to as "her." Let *her* have *her* perfect work, so faith and patience work together.

If Randy Shankle comes under attack, my wife, Gloria, comes right up alongside of me and begins to support or stabilize or secure me. She is a good stabilizer, a good helpmeet. She may be sitting there, we will say, somewhat inactive, but bring her husband under attack, and she gets activated. She is highly activated! She worketh! She will come to my aid and assistance to stabilize me, to see to it that I do not get abused or hurt, or that somebody does not "jump on my case." She does it without even thinking. That is her nature.

That is what happens when my faith comes under fire. Immediately patience comes to the aid and assistance of what I believe in order to stabilize me. Consistency comes right up there if my soul is in submission. About 1973, I was learning this and found out that, thank God, I *am* healed by the stripes of Jesus. The next thing I knew, here came the devil to bring sickness upon me.

So then faith cometh by hearing, and hearing by the word of God (Rom. 10:17). The Word comes, faith comes, Satan comes. That is all we have ever known, and the Word of God does teach things in that order. The Word comes, faith comes, and Satan comes immediately to steal the Word. Well, we have to go further. The Word comes, our faith comes, Satan comes to test your faith to see if you really believe what you say you believe. However, when Satan comes, patience (*hupomone*) comes, and consistency comes. Consistency or patience will produce a work of experience, and experience worketh hope. (Rom. 5:4.)

. . . We glory in tribulations also; knowing that tribulation worketh patience; and patience, experience . . . . (Rom. 5:3,4). In other words, if you let patience work and work long enough, she will bring you experience. What type of experience? A bad experience? No. The bad experiences come when you do not let patience have her perfect work. Your faith will not stay constant, your thought processes will not be under control, and you are going to have an experience independent and opposite to the Word of God. You then will formulate a reason, saying, "Well, the reason this happened is because God doesn't want to do this and this and this." Remember, that thought is fertile. If you don't bring that thought into captivity, it will become a fortified wall, then a way of life, and you become "computerized." Every time you come to the same area, you will respond the same way. You have a stronghold that will have to be pulled down some-day, because you accepted an experience as a theological belief. Wrong thoughts bring wrong beliefs, and you are held captive by wrong reasoning.

Someone will have to come in with the Word of God, refute that belief, challenge that thinking, tear it down, and re-establish the fact that you missed it. The real reason you did not experience all that God promised was because you did not remain constant to His Word. All you have to do is look at the Book of

Revelation and see how many times the word *overcomer* is used. What does overcomer mean? It means, "Stay with it until you win." There are a lot of people whose faith is made shipwreck. If you don't stay with it, you are not going to make it. That principle operates in every area of life.

The Word comes, faith comes, Satan comes, and patience comes, which brings experience, which brings hope. That is the way it should operate. **In your patience possess ye your souls** (Luke 21:19). Why? Because it is in the soulish realm that Satan brings doubt and unbelief regarding the healing power of God in your life. I tell you what, it was amazing to me when I got hold of the revelation of this thing, and it will be amazing to you as well.

Satan Comes to Steal the Word

Satan came immediately to try to steal the revelation of healing from me, and within the next day or two, I woke up sick, but I got out of bed because I had the revelation. I counted it a joy, not the sickness, but what I *knew* brought me joy. I knew that the trying of my faith puts to work the force of consistency which is going to control my soul, to keep my soul from saying, "Well, I *thought* I was well. I *thought* I was healed. I thought this stuff worked like God's Word said." No, I am weaned from all that. I finally grew up and found that God meant what He said and said what He meant. When He said you were healed, you *were* healed!

I got out of bed, walked into the living room, got on my knees, and said, "God, I want you to know nothing has changed." Consistency was speaking. "I was healed 2,000 years ago. I was healed two weeks ago. I am healed today. I don't care what my body says.

The Word says I'm healed, and my body is going to start aligning with my spirit. My soul is in submission to my spirit, and my spirit will not get outside the Word of God. I am letting consistency *(hupomone)* bring control over my soul, and my spirit is fighting the good fight of faith, and I am going to win the battle right here."

I *was* healed, but Satan came for it. That is why he is called a thief. Why would someone be called a thief if he does not steal what someone else already has? **The thief cometh not, but for to steal, and to kill, and to destroy . . .** (John 10:10). A thief does not take what belongs to him. A thief takes that which legally belongs to somebody else, or he would not be called a thief. Satan came with sickness to remove or steal my health. If my soul had gotten out of control and into fussing and fretting and worrying, and into fear and doubt and unbelief of God, I would have lost my health in exchange for Satan's sickness. He would have stolen my health, and I would have gotten his sickness.

I didn't say, "Well, I'm sick. I guess it didn't work." I had learned better than that. I counted that trial as a joy because my soul was under control. I immediately got released in prayer. That sickness and disease left my body, and I went about my business. The next night, it happened again.

I wanted to be consistent, so I got out of bed, walked over, got on my knees again, lifted my hands, and said, "God, nothing has changed. Hallelujah! I am still healed by the stripes of Jesus Christ." I was healed, and I would not let my soul man get inconsistent. He must stay consistent in the faith walk. Faith is in agreement with the Word, the Word is applied to my spirit, and my spirit says, "I'm healed." I had to be consistent all the way down the line.

The third night, around 3 or 4 a.m., I woke up sick again, got up, prayed, and claimed healing. The fourth night, around the same time, I woke up sick and did the same thing. The fifth night, the same thing happened. Boy, I was getting tired and feeling weary and just wanting to quit. The thought came, "This stuff is not working," so I got out of bed, got on my knees, and started to say, "God, I don't care how I feel." When I started talking, I felt the presence of God. I have had this happen since then on numerous occasions and am finally familiar with how His presence affects me when He comes.

That night, I said, "Oh, I'm going out." When I did, my head and arms went down, and I went limp. My spirit stepped out of my body, walked away perhaps eight feet, then turned and looked back at the body. There I was in spirit form. The thought came to me, "I *really* am a spirit man. That body is just a shell." In other words, I am a spirit who inhabits that body. The body is just a house for the spirit-soul man.

When I looked up, right in front of me were two demon spirits. One was on my left and the other on my right. The one on the left was about six inches taller than I am, a lot bigger, and confident and bold. The one on the right, about my height, was full of fear and trembling. They were very hairy with arms that reached down to about four or five inches from their ankles. Their fingernails were some two to three inches long, black, and curled like a half-moon. The hair was real coarse like that of a pig. There definitely were some differences between their appearance and man's.

I don't want to focus on the graphic details of what they looked like, I just want to tell you what happened. As I stood there, looking at them, not knowing what to do, the big one lifted up his hand. The way he did it was very strange, very different from the way we lift our hands. His arms were so long that he brought his hand up and kind of threw it out with a big, long finger pointing at me. He threw his head back, laughing, and said, "You are wasting your time. We have been sent with a purpose, a commission, and you are wasting your time, for you can't stop it."

The commission they had been given, the purpose for their coming, was to make me sick and get me to deny the Word of God and get me off my consistency. The force of patience had brought control to my soul. He had been weaned up to that point. He had been dealt with by God. He was not going to doubt or argue with God. He was not going to be as the Israelites that complained and wanted their own selfish ways by murmuring, "I'm tired of the manna. Give me the quail." Like children, they said, "I don't want this. I want that. I want a red bike. I want a blue bike." My, my, we need to bring some control to our children, and America won't be so bad. We also need to bring control to our own souls.

The big demon went through his gyrations with all the accusations about, "You are wasting your time, and so on," and I did not quite know what to do. I just stood there watching him. The one on the right was trembling, and the scripture came to my mind, . . . **The devils also believe and tremble** (James 2:19). They fear the authority of Christ in believers.

All of a sudden, I heard this sound coming from far away in the heavenlies. It had the kind of sound a missile coming fast would make. It got louder and louder and then Someone landed right behind me. When He did, He filled that place with a good

159

presence. Immediately, I was convinced that it was Jesus Christ, but I did not look around. I knew He came from the throne of God. He placed His right hand on my left shoulder. When He did, I gasped, "Oh!," at the power of God flowing through my spirit man. I gasped repeatedly, "Oh, oh, oh," reacting to the *zoe*, the eternal life of God permeating my spirit like an uncontrollable channel, just saturating and permeating me.

Then He said this: "My son, hold fast to that which you have." I believe it was Jesus because of the terminology He used and His electrifying presence and because of the anointing He transferred into my spirit man.

What was it I had? I tried to figure out what I had. I looked up at the two spirits and at the bold one who had been haughty and laughing so boastfully just a few minutes before. His sardonic smile was gone. The joke was over. That guy got sober quickly in the presence of Jesus. I am telling you that was quite an experience! The demons didn't think it was so funny anymore.

I thought again, "What do I have?" Then the scripture came, . . . **Hold fast to the confession of your faith, nothing wavering; for he is faithful that promised** (Heb. 10:23). Be consistent to what the faith of God says. Faith always speaks in line with the Word because *faith comes by the Word*, and the Word says we were healed 2,000 years ago. I was to hold fast to what I had, *not* try to get it, because I already had it.

Then I said to the demon, "No, *you* are wasting *your* time. I am healed by the stripes of Jesus Christ. I was healed 2,000 years ago. I am healed now, and nothing has changed, thank God." That is the voice of consistency when the soul refuses to doubt in a time of pressure, under tribulation, under financial pressure, or under physical pressure.

I immediately found that I really knew what I had and that the demons had come to tempt my soul man to become inconsistent in the faith walk so that Satan could rob the Word out of my heart and I would end up sick. I turned, after I told them what Jesus had told me, walked right back to my body, stepped down into it, and got up off the floor. By then, I knew I was back in the old body, back into the world consciousness. My heart was just pounding. Backing up against the wall, I said to those two demons that I could tell were still there, "Nothing has changed. I was healed 2,000 years ago and, even though I am back in my body and can't see you now, nothing has changed. I am healed, and I am going to hold fast to that. My soul is under control. I am going to bed." At that point, I just turned and went back to bed. In doing so, I found that in the Word of God, you must deny yourself the right to selfishness, to all fretting, fussing, murmuring, and complaining about whether or not the Word is true. You must settle, with finality, once and for all, that it is true.

Jesus said, . . . **The words that I speak unto you, they are spirit, and they are life** (John 6:63). He said, . . . **I am the way, the truth, and the life** . . . (John 14:6).

God is not a man, that he should lie; neither the son of man, that he should repent: hath he said, and shall he not do it? Or hath he spoken, and shall he not make it good?

Numbers 23:19

So shall my word be that goeth forth out of my mouth: it shall not return unto me void, but it shall accomplish that which I please,

and it shall prosper in the thing whereto I
sent it.

Isaiah 55:11

That is the engrafted Word (James 1:21) which is
able to save my soul. That is the Word of God about
my body. God told me that my body was healed. It was
the demons who told me it was sick. Who am I going
to believe, God or the devil? I am going to believe God,
through my spirit, not the devil trying to speak through
my soul. My soul is in agreement with my spirit, and
I am saved, thank God! My spirit is saved, my soul is
saved, and I am going to stay in alignment with God's
Word. That is how you control the soul.

The Anchoring of the Soul

What else does the soul need? It needs to be
anchored.

**That by two immutable things, in which it
was impossible for God to lie, we might have
a strong consolation, who have fled for refuge
to lay hold upon the hope set before us:
Which hope we have as an anchor of the soul,
both sure and steadfast, and which entereth
into that within the veil.**

Hebrews 6:18,19

Don't let the ship of the soul go up and down on
the waves. Get settled and sure on the Word of God.
Throw the anchor of hope, the expectation in God,
overboard, and your soul will become relaxed and
secure. Hope is the anchor of the soul.

**For consider him that endured such contradic-
tion of sinners against himself, lest ye be
wearied and faint in your minds.**

Hebrews 12:3

The word *minds* is the word *psuche,* souls. Where do you grow weary? Where do you grow weary of confessing the Word and weary of standing on the Word of God? Do you ever grow weary of believing God? It is your soul man who gets weary and wants to faint. He wants to quit. He wants to draw back, but I have news for you. The Word of God teaches very clearly that you must get your soul anchored. You must get into a place where he does not grow weary and does not faint. This is understanding the psuche or soulish realm:

1. Deny the soul.

2. Wean the soul.

3. Quiet and calm the soul.

4. Control the soul.

5. Anchor the soul and bring him under control so that he will not grow weary and faint. Why? . . . **In due season we shall reap if we faint not** (Gal. 6:9).

It is in the soul man where you cast . . . **away your confidence** (Heb. 10:35). Throw away all the confidence of the Word of God and get into unbelief and doubt, and you lose control of the soul. Deny him, wean him, control him, bring him into a fixed position with the Word of God and into submission to the Bishop of the soul — Jesus.

1 Peter 2:25 says that He is the Shepherd and the Bishop of our souls. The Greek word for bishop is *episkope.* The same word is translated "overseer." We are to be overseers of our souls under Jesus. Deal with the soul correctly and wisely, then you will get weaned and grow up a mature Christian.

Faith says, "Yes, God's Word is true," but hope says, "Someday, we're going to walk in the power of God.

It won't be long." That is our hope. Thank God, I've got hope, and I'm not going to throw it away and let my soul be without an anchor. My hope is in the Word of God. I have anchored myself both sure and steadfast, thank God.

> Which hope we have as an anchor of the soul, both sure and stedfast, and which entereth into that within the veil.

> Whither the forerunner is for us entered, even Jesus, made an high priest forever after the order of Melchizedec.

Hebrews 6:19,20

In other words, if you want to anchor your soul, keep it both sure and steadfast, anchor your thought processes to God's Word because hope is born from the Word. Knowing that God has said something, we believe it. We put our hope in God that someday it is going to come to pass. If I keep my soul anchored, I have the ability to move into His presence, within the veil, because I am not going to murmur. I am not going to complain. What brings you into the presence of God? Faith, trust, confidence. What keeps you out of it? Flesh, unbelief, doubt, worry, fear, anxiety, depression, and oppression will keep you out of the veil.

The soul man wants feelings, but we don't base this on feelings. I have him anchored. I have control over him, so whether he "feels" it or not does not mean a thing. Your feelings will lie to you. Jesus said, "Watch and pray." That is a commandment. It is not optional. Keep constant to the Word of God. Don't lift that anchor and start drifting around trying to find another more comfortable place to land. The storm may be tough, but don't lift up anchor. Stay where you are. Don't move. The Holy Spirit will speak to you and tell you when it is time for the ship to move on with God.

It is so interesting to me that in the great moves of God, when feelings are excited and the emotional man is on a high apex because of the tangible presence and power of God, people come to church all of the time. It is during those times, however, that their spirits get leaner and leaner, which shows you who is where. This attitude shows how much soul is in control of a person's life and how much control he has over his soul. A person's reaction to the moves of God exposes how soulish that person really is. When it looks as if nothing is happening with God is when you need to stay constant and press in to Him. I am staying in the veil, and I am not coming out.

The Overseer of the Soul

In 1 Peter 2:25, it says, **For ye were as sheep going astray;** (What made them go astray? They were led astray by a thought process that was inaccurate.) **but are now returned unto the Shepherd and Bishop of your souls.** The word *bishop* means "overseer." The Greek word for *overseer* is *episcope*. *Epi* means "over," and *skopos* means "scope or vision." *Overseer*, or bishop, then, means someone "to oversee your thought processes, your reasonings, and your logic." Peter was talking about the overseer of the *psuche* — the mind, will, and emotions.

I learned this, and it has been dynamic for me. In a time of waiting, where is God working? He is working inwardly, in a new work, a new direction, a new purpose. Where, then, will the voice come from, within or without, if it is from God? It will come from within. Watch all outward filtering thoughts that come through your mind because the soulish realm is the demonic realm. Watch for outside interference, such as words that may come by what someone else says, or words that bring some thought to your mind. Make sure that the moment that thought comes, you take it to the Word. If it passes the Word, accept it as God.

You can be highly motivated and tempted by the devil to do some things you know God has not spoken about. I am not talking about sin in the area of the Tree of Knowledge of Evil but in the area of the Tree of Knowledge of Good. It is the same fruit, but both areas reproduce death, so don't partake of that which seems "right" or "good," if it is apart from God.

Suppose God's plans for my life will not be ready for two more weeks. What am I going to do? Will I *psuche* out, or get over into the soulish realm and reason? In two weeks, the devil can bring about a lot of havoc if you don't hang tight and do what God's Word says. In less than twenty-four hours, the soul man can get so upset, so uptight that he will sin. He will get mad, murmur, open his mouth and speak against God, and say, "What in the world are You doing?" You have already sinned when you have done that. Just what is God wanting to do? He is wanting to put an overseer over your soul. You are going to have to take the spirit man and the Word of God and let the Word and your spirit be an overseer to watch over your soulish realm and thought processes. If you have never done this with consistent discipline, it needs to be done now. You need to discipline yourself to watch over your thought processes. Govern, sift, and test every thought that comes to your mind. If you do not, you are going to *psuche* out. You are going to get over into the soulish realm and cause some problems for yourself or those around you. You will do it every time.

In the past — and thank God, I have been delivered from this reaction — I have even ripped the shirt off my back because I was so upset that nothing was going on. Everything had been going great, then all of a sudden, God made a move, and I wasn't ready for it. I didn't want it in the first place. God had tried to slow me down and get my attention, but I didn't want to listen. I was walking down the road, angry as could be, and I ripped off my shirt, threw it in the trash can, and said, "There!" What good did that do? All it did was cost me one of my favorite shirts. I acted like a foolish child. Thank God, that was years ago.

If you don't bring oversight to the soul, you will do ridiculous things. You may even go out and tear things up. You must get your thoughts under control, and let God work in you. Set a watchman over your soul. Who is the true Shepherd and Bishop of your soul? Jesus is the Chief Overseer, and the Word and the Holy Spirit are His means of oversight through your spirit, so allow the Word and the Spirit to do their job.

Rest Unto the Soul

The soul also needs a place of rest. I am going to give you two words for *rest* and what they mean. This revelation is so powerful.

> Come unto me, all ye that labour and are heavy laden, and I will give you *rest*.

> Take my yoke upon you, and learn of me; for I am meek and lowly in heart: and ye shall find *rest* unto your souls.

> For my yoke is easy, and my burden (portion) is light.

> **Matthew 11:28-30**

In verse 28, the Greek word translated *rest* means "repose, refresh or tranquil." When the soul comes under pressure, he needs to be tranquilized. This *rest* is where man ceases from his own labors. He has entered into Christ's rest. The struggle is over. There is no more push, pump, and pull, and no more soulish activity to get God to demonstrate or perform. This is the repose of the soul. The myriad activities of programs, ideas, new concepts, church buildings, "hype sells," "heavy promos," etc. have ended. Enter into God's rest — cease from your own labors. Cast the whole of your cares over on Jesus. Cease from the thoughts and plans of how to have a bigger church, a better church, a prettier church, a larger ministry, or a bigger mailing list. Stop all the mental, soulish activity, and enter into God's rest. Let Him perform. You are not the performer. God is both the "promiser" and the "performer."

> He staggered not at the promise of God through unbelief; but was strong in faith, giving glory to God;
>
> And being fully persuaded that, what he had promised, he was able also to perform.
>
> Romans 4:20,21

The second definition for rest is in Matthew 11:29, where *rest* means "intermission or recreation." You shall find "recreation," or an "intermission," unto your soul. Do you know why God gives you intermission unto your soul? If you don't have it, the soul will "tilt." It's called a "nervous breakdown." That is a *psuche* out of control with anxiety and worry. When you say, "My God, I can't take it anymore," suicidal tendencies take hold. You should get hold of your soul before it gets to that point. Otherwise, you will lose it.

God gives His men and women intermissions, places to go where they can have a break from it all, so to speak. I thank God for the moments of intermission — a bike ride, a horseback ride, a little "kicking back" in the woods, or whatever you can do for a time of soulish relaxation — because the soul man cannot stay geared up without a break. That is why men of God have heart attacks at 30 or 40 years of age. That minister has operated too much in the soulish realm and not enough in the spirit, so that his soul man is being taxed with the labor of spiritual work when he ought to enter into Jesus' rest and let Jesus Christ operate through him. His struggle ends where God's spirit begins. He needs to let God do the work through him and just enjoy the whole thing.

I think Christianity is the greatest entertainment, in the sense of rest and relaxation, that my soul man has ever had. I enjoy it. My soul man enjoys it, but he did not used to. He used to try to perform it. Now he just watches the spirit man perform.

The Soul Is to Magnify the Lord

Finally, the soul under control needs to magnify the Lord because if he doesn't, he will magnify his own reasonings. He will magnify himself and exalt himself against the knowledge of God.

> . . . My soul doth magnify the Lord, And my spirit hath rejoiced in God my Saviour.

> **Luke 1:46,47**

The spirit rejoices in God, but the soul has to be taught how to magnify God. You had better teach the soul to magnify God's Word, God's ways, and God's actions. The soul had better magnify the name of Jesus, or it will magnify something else. The soul has a way of exalting things. It exalts self-knowledge, self-wisdom, self-revelation, self-pride, self-everything. You must teach the soul man to magnify what God's Word says.

In other words, I exalt the Word above my reasonings. I exalt the Word that says, **By whose stripes, ye were healed** (1 Pet. 2:24) above what my body says. I exalt the name of Jesus above every name. I have to do that because my soul man wants to exalt the feelings, reasonings, logic, and imaginations that are contrary to God. I refuse to let my soul say, "I'm in so much pain I'll never get healed." I refuse to believe that because the Word says He healed me with His stripes 2,000 years ago. I *must* magnify that. If I do not, God's Word will not exalt me into health.

Your soul must magnify the Lord, the Word, and His wisdom. You must exalt the knowledge of God above self-knowledge and the humility of God above self-pride. *Exalt God.*

12
HEARING THROUGH WAITING

This chapter contains a revelation that you will need dozens and dozens of times before Jesus returns. This teaching is not something you learn and do, and then it is over. It is something you learn and continue to do in your walk with Jesus.

How many times have there been when you had to wait on God, and it didn't seem as if anything was happening in your life? During those spiritual lulls, when you don't know what is happening, the soul man can get out of hand with reasonings and logic and confuse or deceive you through the work of Satan. The next thing you know, you are off on a tangent somewhere. You come out of the lull with an "Ishmael" instead of the fruit, or the "Isaac," which God intended. You wind up in bondage. It costs you, and you can't figure out what happened. You just live chasing your life and never seem to get ahead or get out of these things.

The Difference Between Acting and Waiting

One of the hardest things for Christians to learn to do is *wait on God*. It is extremely difficult because of the strength of the *psuche* to create, to imagine, to figure out what to do or how to do something. Understanding the conflict in our minds between *acting* and *waiting* will illuminate the area of faith, because faith is acting. The conflict comes because we know that faith demands action.

According to James 1:22, we are to be doers of the Word and not just hearers only, to avoid deceiving ourselves. We have to put corresponding action to faith, or it is not faith at all. Not all Christians understand this aspect of the Word that commands us to act on, perform, and be doers of what we believe.

There is another side of the Word that commands us to "wait on God." It sounds like a contradiction, but it is only a contradiction in terms, not in reality. Some people, however, *rule out waiting on God because of their faith in God*. Others will *rule out faith in God because of their waiting on God*. It is very difficult for the soul man to learn to wait on God. Jesus said, however, that there is a waiting that brings the soulish realm into a place of rest in order to learn the ways of God. This resting place allows God to initiate and create a world for the soul.

Let's consider a question that you are familiar with: "How does faith come?" Faith comes by hearing the Word of God. **So then faith cometh by hearing, and hearing by the word of God** (Rom. 10:17) is one of our basic "faith statements." When does faith begin? It begins when the will of God is known. In dealing with the apparent conflict between acting and waiting, we have to deal with another problem — presumption.

Faith begins where the will of God is known. Faith is acting on the revealed will of God for your life.

> **They rose up early in the morning, and gat them up into the top of the mountain, saying, Lo, we be here, and will go up unto the place which the Lord hath promised: for we have sinned.**

172

And Moses said, Wherefore now do ye transgress the commandment of the Lord? but it shall not prosper.

Go not up, for the Lord is not among you; that ye be not smitten before your enemies.

For the Amalekites and the Canaanites are there before you, and ye shall fall by the sword: because ye are turned away from the Lord, therefore the Lord will not be with you.

But they *presumed* to go up unto the hilltop: nevertheless the ark of the covenant of the Lord, and Moses, departed not out of the camp.

Numbers 14:40-44

Read verse 45 and you will see that the Israelites got whipped. What did they *presume* to do? They presumed to go up without God. Presumption is entirely different than faith. Faith is acting on the Word of God that has come unto you, or the will or Word of God that has been made known unto you. You know *what* to do when God speaks, because of what He has said. You cannot go ahead of God. You must wait to hear from God. It is not of faith if it doesn't come from the Word, and you cannot act if you don't know what to do.

Have you ever been in a place where you don't know what to do, but you feel tremendous pressure to do something? What do you do? You would like to wait, but you don't wait. You get up and do something, after you have lain in bed and figured out what to do. There is great pressure (the Gethsemane place) on the soul when we don't know from God what to do, but want to do something. *The only reason for the pressure*

173

is the soul's desire to do something! Now, if you yield to that pressure and act, is that faith? No, that's presumption! That is going somewhere or doing something without the revealed will of God on what to do, and God is not going with you to back up your presumption.

Mixing Acting and Waiting

We think we have the right to move independently of God. That is the identical mistake that Eve made. Do you see where her mistake wound up and what it got us? We do not have the right to move independently of God even if it seems to be good, even if it seems to be the work of God. . . . **Ye are not your own . . . ye are bought with a price . . .** (1 Cor. 6:19,20). I cannot imagine moving independently of God and going my own way with the Holy Spirit sitting back there saying, "Well, I hope he makes it. I'm going to do my best to preserve him and keep him out of trouble; but, boy, he sure isn't going where I'd go." I wouldn't want to do that.

We must learn to seek God and to wait. We have to learn how to act, and that is what I want to show you how to do. Mix waiting and acting so that you can complement the Word of God through obedience. When we wait, we bring ourselves to a position of respecting God. We believe in, and are confident of, God. I have waited for divine timing when absolutely nothing seemed to be happening in my life, but I would not presume to go up until I heard from God. You need to learn to wait for God to speak.

Statements such as, "We can't just sit here and do nothing; we've got to do something," lead you into making fatal mistakes. If you don't know what to do, you'd better not do anything. Don't make a move until you know what God wants you to do. Don't act, and call it faith, when there is no Word behind it. That is presumption.

When you don't know what to do, do what you know to do: *Walk in the light that God has revealed to you up to that time.* If He has given you no further light or revelation or direction, don't move. The soul is commanded to wait on God. I know of men and women who have come into a local body knowing that God had a plan and a purpose for them. Some of them came after being directly spoken to by God's spirit, yet they never made it into the purpose He intended.

An Expectancy in the Kingdom of God

May God open your eyes to His purpose. May you know His plan for your life and lay hold of it and seize the moment. This is an expectant moment in the Kingdom of God. The heart of Jesus Christ is overwhelmed with expectancy for His people. He is releasing so much of it because He is so full of it. His expectancy is overflowing into hearts and the lives of those who are walking uprightly with Him and staying in tune with Him. It is dripping out of Him like honey all over His people who are walking close to Him! Tremendous expectancy! Do you know what that expectancy is? It is that God's plans are developing over His Body and in our lives.

The great conflict between acting and waiting is no conflict when you have the light of His Word. I do not initiate, create, or motivate. I wait until God's plans develop further and more light is shed, more revelation is shown, and more doors are open so that I can comprehend where I am going.

You may be in a place of waiting and being prepared for God's plans to develop. If so, you need to respect His plans. Some people will not wait on God's plans to develop. What do they do? They act prematurely. It saddens my heart to know that some have done that. Do you know where they will be when the thrust of God hits? Do you know where they will be when the wave picks up and moves across America? They will be on the outside of it and wondering what happened to them. They will say, "Well, I had the revelation of it. I knew it was coming. I heard the prophecies. I was involved with the teachings. I have heard what was said. I believed it, too. Why wasn't I involved?"

Can you tell me why they were not in the move of God? They would not respect God's plans and wait for them to develop. They had to move in the "now" with their soul realm. They wanted to operate in the realm of faith without the revealed will of God. You can't do it. You can't act on faith without the Word. You must know what sayeth the Spirit and what sayeth the scriptures. When you have the revealed will, you can act your faith. In fact, you had *better* act your faith. You had better get up and act on what you believe and what you know the Word of God says, then watch God's performance in your life.

Until that time, you must wait. I want to emphasize that this is one of the hardest things for people to do — wait on God when they don't know why they're waiting or what to do. Just why are they waiting? Well, now we can answer that. The reason they are waiting is for God's plans to develop. Sometimes we think that God has forsaken us or has forgotten us or that we're not going anywhere or doing anything. "Everybody else seems to be doing something, but I'm not." I went through that until I found how to get in the flow of God.

Wherefore, my beloved, as ye have always obeyed, not as in my presence only, but now much more in my absence, work out your own salvation with fear and trembling:

For it is God which worketh in you both to will and to do of his good pleasure.

Philippians 2:12,13

God is the One working in you, and He is working in you two things: both the *will* and the do; both the revelation of His plan and the performance of it; both the desire of it and the execution of it. You need to be fully persuaded that what God has promised to do, He will perform. (Rom. 4:21.) Have you not seen God change or move that which was difficult in your life?

From the time I was a child, I was known as being too impatient and impulsive. I never learned to be patient, but where sin did abound, grace did abound more abundantly. (Rom. 5:20.) Where I was an impatient man, God has taught me how to be patient and wait on Him. If I had not learned, I would have missed this great wave of God.

You must learn to wait, because I know that God is at work within you, just as He is at work within me, for a divinely instituted purpose. The soul that does not learn to wait on God in expectation always will resist divine timing, because he is full of energy, creativity, ability, the desire to exercise his own will, and the desire to initiate things. It is the spirit of a man that should initiate things in a man's life, not the soul. The soul is not to move independently of God. He must wait on God to speak to his spirit, and then he will move *with* God, not before God speaks to him.

The Post of Observation

In *The Amplified Bible* translation of Habakkuk 2:1-3, it says:

> . . . I will [in my thinking] stand upon my post of observation, and station myself on the tower or fortress, and will watch to see what He will say within me, ... (*Within* you refers to your spirit man. He is saying, "And I will watch in my soul to see what He will say to my spirit man.") and what answer I will make [as His mouthpiece] to the perplexities of my complaint against Him.

> And the Lord answered me, and said, Write the vision, and engrave it so plainly upon tablets that every one who passes may be able to read [it easily and quickly] as he hastens by.

> For the vision is yet for an appointed time, and it hastens to the end [fulfillment]; it will not deceive or disappoint. Though it tarry, wait [earnestly] for it; because it will surely come, it will not be behindhand on its appointed day.

> **Habakkuk 2:1-3**

The prophet is simply saying here, "I am going to set myself up on the post of observation." That is hearing from God through waiting on God. There are times we must hear from God on certain issues, but in a spiritual lull, it seems as if He is not answering, speaking, directing, or moving. Do you know why? It is because the cloud that directs by day has stopped. (Ex. 13:21.) In Exodus 40:34-38, Moses related that when the cloud moved, the Israelites moved with it. When the cloud stopped, they stopped and pitched their tents.

There are times in each individual's life when he needs to remain where he has pitched his tent. That does not mean he isn't going to get answers to prayers for the basics of life, but it does mean he is not going to get a lot of understanding or direction because God is not directing. The cloud is not moving. In that place of a pitched tent, you can get your needs met and your body healed and delivered. You can lay hands on the sick and the power and anointing will be present, for that is His will on any occasion, but when the Holy Spirit begins to move a Body of believers, individually or collectively, to a new place, things are different. The Lord led Israel by a pillar of fire by night and a cloud of the glory of God by day, and when that cloud rested, they rested. They pitched their tents and drove their stakes down. Sometimes it was less than twenty-four hours, and sometimes it was weeks before the cloud moved again.

A lady evangelist came up to me in a meeting once. I have a kindred spirit with this lady, and every time I get around her she says, "Randy, tell me what God is saying. I want to hear what the Holy Spirit is speaking." She is comparing notes with what He speaks to me and what He speaks to her. She is "confirming" the Word. This particular time, here is what I told her the Holy Spirit had revealed to me:

"Well, we are stepping out of the confined, restricted, limited realm over into a large room with

God, but He told me that with every move of God, there comes an encounter with resistance that demands a confrontation with persistence."

She just looked at me, amazed, and said, "My goodness, listen to what He has told me." It was much the same, except for a few variations: "With every move of God, it will come to an end, and it will die. When it dies, it formulates two kinds of people, those who go on with God, and those who refuse to go. Those who refuse to go on become the critics and persecutors of those who do."

I began looking at that pattern all the way back down the line. Do you know who the Pentecostals got all the criticism from? It came from fundamentalists who pitched their tents and camped before the cloud moved on to the baptism of the Holy Spirit. Do you know who the Pentecostals became critics of? They criticized the Charismatics. Do you know who many Charismatics will criticize? They will be the critics of those Christians who are involved in the next move of God. I want to encourage you not to camp with any group but to go with God.

It seems that every great move of God comes to a temporary stop so that, before He goes on, everything that can be shaken will be shaken. (Heb. 12:27.) It is then that we find out who will believe God and go on and who will not. It is a time of proving the heart to find out if you really believe what God says.

Wait — Listen — Speak

God says three things in the first verse of Habakkuk 2, in the *Amplified:*

1. **I will stand upon my post of observation.** (I will wait.)

2. **To see what He will say within me.** (I'm going to listen to God.)

3. **What answer I will make.** (I'm going to speak for God.)

It was not until *after* he heard from God that he spoke. When you begin to wait on God, it is the soul man that has a great desire to start something. "I have to get out of this thing somehow. I have to do something," he will say. I have heard that a lot of times. I have also heard the other question that comes up at these times, "What are you going to do now?" Who is tempting you to do something? That temptation comes from the devil. Has God spoken at that time? If He hasn't, you had better not do anything. You had better stay on the post of observation and keep your outlook and vision going with God. Keep watching over your soul, and see to it that you wait and listen until God does speak. Then you can move because the Word says that **faith cometh by hearing, and hearing by the Word of God** (Rom. 10:17).

How do you get prosperity? You put the Word into your heart and in your mouth, and meditate on it day and night. If you are not doing that, you are operating in presumption.

> **This book of the law shall not depart out of thy mouth; but thou shalt meditate therein day and night, that thou mayest observe to do according to all that is written therein: for then thou shalt make thy way prosperous, and then thou shalt have good success.**
>
> **Joshua 1:8**

Once I hear from the Lord, faith cometh, and when faith cometh, I can act on what I have heard and say,

181

"In the name of Jesus, this is what God has told me to do. This is what the Holy Spirit says, and this is what is going to happen." Until I hear, I have learned to wait, for He says, **My son, attend to my words; incline thine ear unto my sayings** (Prov. 4:20). The word *incline* means "to lean toward." Don't do anything until you hear from God. In a time of pressure, I used to initiate things. Each time, I would come up with an "Ishmael," and when it was all over with, I would have to work my way out of that thing somehow.

One of the problems with communication between people is semantics, or a word meaning one thing to one person and another to someone else. One clear definition of *waiting*, however, is "to remain expecting something." That does not mean just kicking back and trying to get through this thing the best way you can. It doesn't mean being resigned to the situation or giving up and saying, "Well, I hope this thing gets over somehow and something happens some way." No. You need to be waiting with an expectancy that something is going to happen favorably on your behalf, with the knowledge that God has not forgotten you.

Years ago, when it didn't look as if anything was happening in my life, the Holy Spirit began to speak to me in a meeting one night. He said, "I haven't put you on a shelf to collect dust." I have always remembered that. He has never put me on a shelf. He has never put you aside and later said, "Oh, what was your name? What was it I promised to do in your life? Let me see if I can remember that. Jesus, can you help me remember?" Jesus has never said, "I don't know either."

God is ever mindful of us. He knows exactly where we are, so I take confidence in what faith really is. **Now**

faith is the substance (title deed) **of things hoped for, the evidence of things not seen** (Heb. 11:1). Faith is all the proof I need. God said it, I believe it, and that is it! That is where faith really is.

Two things bother me about the Body of Christ when talking about living by faith. They say they are living by faith and trusting Him, but I say, "Give me the Word." If you don't have the Word, you have no faith. That is how faith comes. You don't get up and do the things of God until He speaks, because faith doesn't come until He speaks. I hear these "confessions": "I'm just going to get up and move." "I'm going to do so-and-so." "I'm going to get that job." "I'm going to believe God to bless me." Well, did He tell you to do that? If He didn't, it's not faith.

The other thing that disturbs me is the request to "pray for so-and-so. He is in full-time ministry, and he's just living by faith." The speaker sounds as if that is some type of low, degrading thing to live by. I want you to know, full-time ministry or not, you had better all be living by faith. You had better all learn how to trust and believe God.

13

THE WAITING OF THE SOUL

There are five ways in which God tells us to wait. You need to know these. They are precious.

1. Wait earnestly.
2. Wait patiently.
3. Wait quietly.
4. Wait continually.
5. Wait only.

Wait Earnestly

Do you know what is going on in your heart and your life right now in the eyes of God? He is developing plans for you. He already has laid a vision and prospect out there for you. If you have done what Habbakuk said (see Chapter 12) and heard God speak, then He has told you where you are going, what He is going to be doing, and what to expect. He has given you a vision. How do you wait for the fulfillment of it? You *earnestly* wait.

Then believed they his words; they sang his praise.

Then soon forgat his works; they waited not for his counsel.

Psalm 106:12,13

What did they not wait for? They did not wait for His counsel and instruction. *The Amplified Bible* translates those verses this way:

Then [Israel] believed His words — trusting in, relying on them; they sang His praise.

But they hastily forgot His works; they did not [earnestly] wait for His plans [to develop] respecting them.

The word *earnest* means "serious in purpose or effort; sincere, diligent, and determined." Somebody who is earnestly waiting on God is serious about the purpose and effect of God. People like that are very diligent to take oversight and are determined to see that God's plans and purposes for their lives are established. Are you serious about God's plans developing on your behalf? Are you determined to see that whatever God is planning and purposing for you is going to come to pass? Then you can be fully persuaded that what God has promised, He is able also to perform.

Being confident of this very thing, that he which hath begun a good work in you will perform it until the day of Jesus Christ.

Philippians 1:6

I am confident of that. God's plans for our lives and ministries are dynamic. He is developing them, and I am going to respect them and earnestly wait for them. I respect the purpose of God for my life. I respect God enough, and trust and rely on Him enough, to earnestly wait and watch His plans develop on my behalf. I can wait and watch Him execute His purposes.

It is people who do not earnestly wait for God who move out without a developed plan. They don't know where they are going. They are like "a blind dog in a meat house," just wandering around not knowing what their purposes are or their directions. They do not know what they are doing. They come up with a new plan every week, They say, "Well, that didn't work. I'll think of something else."

What are you going to do? You had better do nothing until God speaks. Wait earnestly until His plans are fully developed. How does God develop His plans? He reveals first the blade, then the ear, after that, the full corn. (Mark 4:28.) You must wait until the full corn comes. I know that there is an expectancy in your heart, but do you have absolute clarity? Release the confession of faith and say:

"I can see it. I can see God's plans, and they are developing right now. He is developing a place to bring me into that purpose, to experience everything He has promised. I will earnestly wait for it to develop and respect it."

The preparations of the heart in man, and the answer of the tongue, is from the Lord.

Proverbs 16:1

It is when a man hears from God that He can truly speak for God. If you speak before you hear, you are speaking presumptuously. God will prepare the heart for His purpose. Don't panic. Don't blow it. Hang tight. Keep trusting God. Keep believing. Don't murmur, don't complain, and don't talk about the problem. Don't magnify the pollution. Exalt the solution: *His name is Jesus.* If you will attend to the precious, the vile will just fall away. I have learned not to get involved in the vile by saying, "My God, I wish something would happen!" Do you know where that will lead you? **They hastily forgot His works; they did not [earnestly] wait for His plans [to develop] respecting them** (AMP) **. . . And he gave them their request; but sent leanness into their soul** (Ps. 106:13,15).

186

Every time I got over into that realm, I stopped waiting for God's plans to develop. I started initiating my own plans, but I found out that I would rather have a developed plan than an undeveloped deception. You are going to go a whole lot farther on God's developed plan than you will with some initiated psuche display. Learn these steps in waiting and acting:

I am on my Post of Observation.

I am going to wait and listen until I hear.

When I hear, I am going to speak for God.

Then I am going to act or move on what I have heard.

That is faith in its best order. **For God speaketh once, yea twice** (Job 33:14). How many times is He going to speak? He speaks twice. **Yet man perceiveth it not. In a dream, in a vision of the night, when deep sleep falleth upon men, in slumberings upon the bed** (Job 33:14,15). God is not limited. He has a lot of ways to contact you. Dreams or visions are two of the ways. If you wait upon your post of observation, **then he openeth the ears of men, and sealeth their instruction** (Job 33:16).

If you have earnestly waited on God, your faith is in gear. You are trusting God, saying, "I haven't heard anything. I don't know what I am supposed to do just yet, God, but I know Your Word says that if I earnestly wait on Your plans to develop, if I continue to be very determined to hear from You before I do anything, then this could be the very night when I lay down to sleep and you open my ear and seal that instruction. I may be able to rise up tomorrow morning with a mouth full of the Word of God and be able to once again say, "The Lord God hath spoken. What could I do but prophesy?"

187

Do you know why you can prophesy and speak the Word of God? You earnestly waited for Him to speak. You were on your post of observation. If you get down on a fleshly level, into the soulish realm, you are not going to be on the tower to see what God is doing.

This type of teaching speaks to our souls and brings them into perspective. This is how the Holy Spirit chastises and corrects His sons. People ask me all the time, "Doesn't God chastise and rebuke and correct?" Yes, He does, but He doesn't use sickness. He uses His Word. Right now, what you are reading is bringing correction and reproof and chastisement to your soul man. He probably doesn't want to hear it. He is saying, "I'm tired of waiting. I'm tired of trusting God. I've been doing this now for twenty-four hours!" He is a heavy weight, isn't he? God will, in spite of your soul, open your ears and seal the instructions of God **that he may withdraw man from his purpose** (Job 33:17). Why does He seal His instructions? Why is He developing and working out His works, desire, and plan in your life? He is working out His purpose, and if you will wait, He will develop that purpose and seal the instruction to the fulfillment of that purpose. Then He will keep you from your own *psuche* pride and your own self-life.

> **That He may withdraw man from his purpose, and hide pride from man.**
>
> **He keepeth back his soul from the pit, and his life from perishing by the sword.**
>
> **Job 33:17,18**

He will keep your *psuche* man from going the way of hell, that which is earthly, sensual, and demonic.

God is not going to speak to your carnal ears. He opens the spirit man, the candle of the Lord. **Thy word is a lamp unto my feet, and a light unto my path** (Ps. 119:105). **The entrance of thy words giveth light** (Ps. 119:130). He takes His precious Word and speaks it to the spirit of a man. The Word is light, the spirit being the candle. God lights that candle, illumination goes on, and you understand the purpose and the direction of God. You can move with surety, if you earnestly wait for God's plan to be developed.

Waiting is for the soul man. He is going to have to earnestly wait on God, respecting God's plans while they are developing, and shut his mouth.

Wait Patiently

There is a way of the world that prospers. Don't fret because of those who look as if they are getting everything right now. Proverbs says the wealth they get now will be of no gain, and another man shall spend it, but Ecclesiastes says man shall **enjoy the good of all his labor** (Eccle. 3:13, 5:18). One kind of man gets wealth and is robbed. Another kind of man makes it by God's way and gets to preserve it by faith, so that the devil can't get it. Which one do you want to be?

Trust in the Lord, and do good; so shalt thou dwell in the land, and verily thou shalt be fed.

Delight thyself also in the Lord; and he shall give thee the desires of thine heart.

Commit thy way unto the Lord; trust also in him; and he shall bring it to pass.

And he shall bring forth thy righteousness as the light, and thy judgment as the noonday.

Rest in the lord, and *wait patiently* for him: fret not thyself because of him who prospereth in his way, because of the man who bringeth wicked devices to pass.

Psalm 37:3-7

The Hebrew word for *wait* is *chiyl* (kheel) meaning "to twist or whirl in a circular or spiral manner; to dance also as in pain, to writhe in pain." It is translated in numerous instances as "to wait patiently," waiting in a circular motion. *Patiently* is the same Hebrew word so that *wait patiently* in the Hebrew is actually one word and means that you are "waiting as in a circular motion or manner." It means "to twirl around and around and around." Just stay with God until He speaks. Stay in that little circle until He speaks. Don't do anything or initiate anything, but when God speaks, break out and go in the direction He gives you.

How do you wait patiently? You must keep the soul confined and restricted. The Word says to keep the soul "as in pain." Do you know what that means? It means "agony of the soul." Your soul will say, "I've been in this thing now for a month, two months, and nothing has happened. Doesn't He know I've got a problem? It looks as if nothing is happening." The pain of the soul comes, but you say, "Shut up, in the name of Jesus. Not my will, but Thine be done. I am going to wait upon (earnestly wait on) God, respecting His plans because I believe they are being fully developed right now on my behalf. He is not leaving me this way. He is not going to cast me off. He is not going to forsake me."

You can relax. God is not going to push you aside. You are going to get your needs met and your stomach fed. He is going to take care of you. Quit taking thought about your life, what you're going to eat, and what you're going to wear. (Matt. 6:25.) God says, "Don't think about it. Cast that thought down." Therefore, I do just that, in the name of Jesus. Keep yourself confined to a limited, restricted realm of thinking during this time, and that is: "I'm going to wait on God until He speaks." How do you wait? You wait patiently.

Wait Quietly

Faith is for the spirit. Hope is for the soul, as we have talked about earlier in this book. Faith says, "Now." Hope says, "Someday." The spirit man says, "I've got it." The soul man says, "I wish you did." **The Lord is my portion, saith my soul** (*nephesh* in the Hebrew, and *psuche* in the Greek) **therefore will I hope in him** (Lam. 3:24).

You must say, "Soul man, I am talking to you. God is your portion." **The Lord is good unto them that wait for him, to the soul that seeketh him. It is good that a man should both hope and *quietly wait* for the salvation of the Lord** (Lam. 3:25,26). This scripture says that a man should wait quietly. Is the writer referring to the spirit, soul, or body of a man? He is referring to the soul man. It is good that my *psuche*, my *nephesh*, my soul man both hopes and not just waits, but waits quietly. The word *quietly* and the word *wait* are *one Hebrew word*. Look at the definition. *Damam* is the word, and it means "still, silent, or to stop."

> Surely I have calmed and quieted my soul, like a weaned child with his mother; like a weaned child is my soul within me [ceased from fretting].

> Psalm 131:2 AMP

In studying this concept of weaning the soul man in the *merismos* teaching years ago, I concluded that it doesn't take very long. Isaiah 28:9 says, **Whom shall he teach knowledge? and whom shall he make to understand doctrine? them that are weaned from the milk, and drawn from the breasts.** The soul man is just like a baby who wants the comfort of the flesh, warm milk, and his mother. The Word says you are going to have to wean him sometime.

You know how fretful babies are when they are being weaned. They cry and want their own way. What people do a lot of times instead of weaning them is give them a pacifier, which only prolongs the weaning. That which is natural comes first, then afterward that which is spiritual. What you are going to have to do is get quiet. In other words, that soul man wants to scream at a time like this and say, "The bills are coming in, and I don't have a job, and I don't know what is coming. It doesn't look as if anything is going on with God."

Your soul wants to do something, but you had better shut that stuff up. It will get hold of you and lead you out of that little circle of patiently waiting on God. You are going to initiate something. Your soul is going to blow it. The self-life will come up with a million things to initiate. If God has told you to do something, for goodness sake, do it, but wait until you hear from God. Those committed to the purpose of God are going to be those who carry the ball when the Spirit moves again. They are going to be out there doing the will of God.

There are two things the Lord told the lady evangelist, whom I mentioned in the last chapter, that the Word confirms: (1) There is the laying **aside every weight, and** (2) **the sin that doth so easily beset us**

(Heb. 12:1). **Which doth so easily beset** is one word in the Greek, *euperistatos*, which means "to take a participator and make him a spectator."

Those who do not know how to control their souls and get the *merismos* teaching down in their spirits, where it can become a reality, are going to have trouble. They will be the murmurers and the complainers who walk around and say, "Well, I don't know what we are going to do. I've heard this, and I've heard that, and I'm getting tired of hearing that." That person has a problem. He is already "*psuche-ing* out" and his soul man is not waiting on God. Although God's plans are being developed on his behalf, he is not going to have any part in them because he is way over to the left or right.

It takes discipline to set a watchman on your lips and make sure that everything that comes out is of God, or not to speak at all. The soul is so opinionated. He thinks he knows everything. You are no different than I was. The soul is the soul until he goes through a metamorphosis. If he does not get changed in his thinking, he has all the views, ideas, and philosophies of the world. He comes up with all the ways and things he can to create and instruct and get it together. Quiet that guy and keep waiting on God.

What is tough on the ego is when someone says, "Well, what is God doing?", and you have to say, "I don't know." It's tough to say that, but if you don't know, say so. Then people will ask, "Well, what are you doing?" You should say, "I am waiting on God's plans to be developed in my life. I am earnestly waiting, and I respect them. I am confident that He is working on my behalf, because, you see, I know the thoughts that my Father thinks toward me. They are thoughts of good and not of evil *to give me an established end."* That means that He has in mind a fulfilled purpose, and I can have absolute security. That is what God is thinking toward you, so get your soul under control and get him quietly waiting on the Lord, still and silent.

Have you ever just put the brakes on him one time? If you say, "Whoa," to your soul, you will find out right away how much control you have over him. You will see how much reigning power the spirit man has. The soul wants to just keep right on going and fighting and resisting and complaining.

You say, "Well, my psychologist said to just go ahead and scream it out." Throw the psychology away, and get back to the Word, because you are about to be snared by the words of your mouth. Wait *earnestly.* Wait in a small, circular manner, *patiently.* Wait *quietly,* which means you still and silence the soul man. You shut him up, continue to wait on God, and you wean him and stop the fretting and the wringing of the hands.

Wait Continually

Continually means "constantly continual." It also has the implication of "stretching itself continually." How long do you wait? You just keep stretching it. Do I have to stretch out the waiting period? Yes, I just stretch it until the plans develop. You say, "I'm tired of waiting." No, stretch it. Wait continually and constantly, by stretching. If I have to stretch it out another week, I am able to do it, aren't you? I can wait on God earnestly, expecting His plans to develop, respecting them. What does that mean?

Therefore turn thou to thy God: keep mercy and judgment, and *wait* on thy God *continually.*

Hosea 12:6

The word *wait* here is the Hebrew word *qarah*, which means "to bind together, to collect, or to gather together." A slang term for this concept would be, "Just pull it together, brother, it is going to be all right."

You may say, "But I feel as if I am falling apart."

Just pull it all together, and continue to group your thoughts all together. Get them continually in line with the Word of God, and keep your emotions grouped up tightly together. That is how you wait. If you feel as if you are about to crack, just pull your emotions together and stretch them out a little farther. You can make it.

You must take the mind, will, and emotions, the thoughts, imaginations, reasoning, and logic, and group them in line with the Word. Keep them tightly related to the Word. Keep your will (the determining factor), your desires, your affections, and your ambitions, tightly grouped to God's Word. Then keep your emotional man stabilized to the Word of God, continually. If you have to wait a little longer, stretch it.

Look at what the Word says. **Therefore turn thou to thy God: keep mercy and judgment, and wait** (Hos. 12:6). Pull it all together around God, continually. Turn the mind to God, turn the will to God, and turn the emotions to God. Stabilize the soulish man. Keep him grouped and knitted around the Word. The Word says, **If you faint in the day of adversity, thy strength is small** (Prov. 24:10). I don't want to faint in the day of adversity. My strength is not small. I am strong in the Lord and in the power of His might. My God never wearies or grows faint.

If thou hast run with the footmen, and they have wearied thee, then how canst thou

195

contend with horses? and if in the land of
peace, wherein thou trustedst, they wearied
thee, then how wilt thou do in the swelling
of Jordan?

Jeremiah 12:5

You are in the land of peace. If you get weary and
can't stretch it very far and wait very long, the prophet
is saying, "How are you going to do if it gets tough."
He is talking about a land of peace. He is talking about
running with your peer group, the footmen, but God
is developing us to run with the horses. We are going
to do what Elijah did — outrun all the chariots. (1 Kings
18:46.) We will just leave them all, thank God. We will
run for forty days, and when the horses faint with
exhaustion and die, we will just keep right on going.
Why? Because we are living by the manna of God, the
Living Bread. We are living by the *zoe*, the life of God.
We are not going to grow weary and faint. God's Word
is nigh us, even in our hearts and in our mouths. Isn't
that good to know? I learned that a few years ago, and
I got rid of my self-pity problem.

You may say, "Yeah, but it's been tougher on me
that on most of them." **There hath no temptation taken
you but such as is common to man** (1 Cor. 10:13). "Well,
I tell you, this is the strangest thing I've ever seen."
**Beloved, think it not strange concerning the fiery trial
which is to try you, as though some strange thing happened unto you** (1 Pet. 4:12). We are not going to give
the soul man any slack. He is going to shut up quickly,
earnestly, and patiently wait until His Daddy speaks.
When He does, then let the soul man have a little
freedom. Let him say, "I told you my Daddy was going
to do it." Let him boast a little, but in God not himself.

196

Wait Only

Say this, "My soul, I'm talking to you now. You be quiet and listen."

My soul *wait* thou *only* upon God; for my expectation is from him.

He only is my rock and my salvation: he is my defense; I shall not be moved.

In God is my salvation and my glory: the rock of my strength, and my refuge, is in God.

Trust in him (sometimes?) at all times; ye people, pour out your heart before him: God is a refuge for us. Selah.

Psalm 62:5-8

Look at the word *wait* in verse 5: **My soul, wait thou only upon God.** It is the Hebrew word *damam*. It comes from the root word which we used in *wait quietly*. The same word, *still, silent* and it means "to stop and wait quietly." Look at the word *only*. The Hebrew word is *ak* which means "surely or by limitation." Say to the soul, "Wait thou only." In other words, "Stop surely, with limitation. Soul man, I'm going to stop you right now! I restrict you with limitations and I limit you to surely (to God only)."

The only thing my soul man is going to wait on is God, and that is the limit of that situation. Stop on God only! Stop with God. He is enough! The soul man doesn't need anything but God. I know he doesn't want to hear that. We need to get to the place where the Word of God means more to us than our opinions, the place where we believe God's opinion is more important than ours and what He says is more important than what we say.

197

Speak the word only, and my servant shall be healed (*Matt. 8:8*). *Thank God, He didn't speak anything else, but that was the only thing He needed to speak. Was the servant healed? Yes, the Word was sufficient. It always is. The Word of God is plenty.*

"Wait thou only, 'psuche man.' You shut up! Stop! You are limited right now. I'm not going to lend your ears to anything else. I'm not going to let you listen to voices. I'm not going to let you listen to circumstances and situations. You turn yourself to God. You listen to God only, and you wait on Him. You stop and limit yourself right now to God only because He is a surety of a better covenant."

It takes some discipline and the work of God. It may take some time, but you are going to have to start somewhere. I found out one thing that the soul man needs more than anything else. He needs God and the Word of God. You must receive with meekness the engrafted Word which is able to save your soul (*psuche*) (James 1:21). Your soul needs to be saved. It will give you a whole lot less trouble in a time when you don't understand everything, or when reasoning and imagination run rampant, saying, "Oh, my God, we may all be dead by tomorrow!" You can answer, "No, you will not!"

Discipline depends on whether you attend to the precious or to the vile. It depends on where your life is. I say to my soul, "Soul, you must wait on God and listen to the Father. Then you speak once He seals the instruction in my spirit, and don't you speak before. You have nothing to say until God speaks."

Here is how I wait. I wait earnestly with a determined expectancy from God, that He has not forgotten me, that He is going to do exactly what He said

He would do. I wait patiently, in a confined realm. I don't get outside of this little realm until God speaks. I don't move presumptuously and try to initiate something, then hope God will bless it. I stay until He speaks. I wait quietly and shut my soul man up. I say, "Shut up. I don't want to hear from your thoughts, reasonings, imaginations, or feelings. I want to hear from God, because I am listening *only* to God."

Then I wait continually. I collect all areas of the soulish man around me, keep it knitted tight, and I continue to wait and continue and continue.

What if the answer does not come? Then I stretch it. I will *wait only*. I will wait for no other than God.

You must listen to the Word because, if you don't, you will listen to something or someone else. You will conclude, "It takes too much hassle to always correct what I say." You are going to say something anyway. It might as well be the Word of God. You may hear yourself say, "I get so tired of hearing, 'That is a bad confession.' " If you correct and change what you say, you probably won't hear that.

It Surely Will Come

In Habakkuk 2:1, he says that he would set himself on a tower and watch to see what the Lord will say unto him, and what he would answer. Notice that in the next two verses, God is about to speak, **and the Lord answered me.** Do you believe that? Do you believe that when you lay down at night, and your head hits the pillow, and you go into a dream or vision, that the Holy Spirit is going to open your ears and seal His instructions? You may as well put your faith in that, because it is the Word. **The Lord answered me!**

I like what Jeremiah says. I say it all the time. He said, **Then the word of the Lord came unto me, saying** (Jer. 1:4). That is my confession. During a time of waiting on God to speak, I say, "Thank God, the Word has come unto me saying. It has come unto me, thank God, in the name of Jesus. I am as persistent as Daniel. It is coming to me, thank God! It is coming to me."

Wait on God. He will come to you. Habakkuk says, **And the Lord answered me, and said, write the vision, and make it plain upon tables, that he may run that readeth it** (Hab. 2:2). In other words, make it so obvious that when anybody passes by, it is going to be clear what God is doing. When God speaks, He will bring clarity to the vision. When He does, let the whole world, the whole universe, know. Make it clear what you are expecting from God, a full display of power and glory. Don't be ashamed of it. Believe it.

> **For the vision is yet for an appointed time, but at the end it shall speak, and not lie: though it tarry** (if it should tarry, what do you do?) *wait for it;* **because it will surely come, it will not tarry.**
>
> **Habakkuk 2:3**

Though it does tarry, or seem to be delayed, go ahead and wait for it because **it will surely come.** It will not delay itself beyond its purpose. It won't be off so long that you faint and can't make it. God has given me a vision to walk and operate in the power and the glory of God. I want my soul and everyone else to hear of it. I have a vision from God that there is a shockwave of power coming. He is going to take the land. He is going to put it in the hands of the righteous. The wealth of the sinner is laid up for you and me (Prov. 13:22), and if they are not just, it is for us. Thank God.

God has told us to take the land. All that you can see, **Every place that the sole of your foot shall tread upon, that have I given unto you** (Josh. 1:3). I see souls saved, home meetings flourishing all over the place, consuming the land. I am interested about the Kingdom of God, because I trust and earnestly wait for God. I wait *patiently* on Him; I *wait only* on Him. I know my God is going to speak and, when He does, you will see that the vision was true.

I like what the prophet said, **Behold now, there is in this city a man of God, and he is an honourable man; all that he saith cometh surely to pass** . . . (1 Sam. 9:6). When will it come to pass? All you have to do is wait and watch and see, for it will surely come. It will not be prolonged forever. What God has spoken, He will also perform because He is going to watch over every word to see that it comes to pass. Every prophecy will come to pass. Not one jot or tittle that God has spoken from the day He began to prophesy shall fall to the ground and be void. It shall not return to Him void, but will accomplish that which He pleases. (Isa. 55:11.) I am encouraged to wait on God.

Prayer

My heavenly Father, I earnestly wait for your plans to develop, and I respect them. I respect the plans because I respect the Planner. I respect what you say. I am not a doubter, I'm not a murmurer or a complainer. God, I am a believer. I believe that it will be unto me even as it was spoken. I know, Father, that Your plans are being established, developed, and perfected. You are preparing us for a purpose, and I thank you that Your purpose is a full display of God in the land. In Jesus' name. Amen."

PART III
THE UNITING OF THE HEART

14
THE DIVIDED HEART

Now I want to deal with knowledge that will give revelation on how the Holy Spirit operates in our lives. Look at Proverbs 4:20-22.

My son, attend to my words; incline thine ear unto my sayings.

Let them not depart from thine eyes; keep them in the midst of thine heart.

For they are life unto those that find them, and health to all their flesh.

The forces of life that come out of the heart are the powers that change and alter things. I want you to look very closely at the next verse because it makes things very clear. **Keep thy heart with all diligence; for out of *it* are the issues** (forces) **of life** (Prov. 4:23). The issues of life are the things that bring a force or power behind them.

The word *keep* here means "to preserve or protect one's desires or aspirations, delights, or passions." The reason for *keeping* your heart is that anytime your affections, passions, or desires are divided, you lose the potential of force for change and alteration of things. The only force that will change your world, future, and destiny is eternal life — *zoe*.

Zoe is the only force that will change behavior because it will change the nature from which behavior comes. What the Church has done for years is preach the gospel to change and alter with the wrong force.

Religious tradition tries to change behavior and attitudes without changing your nature. Even if traditional teaching brought changes, it only changed conduct, not the nature.

Four words are used for *life* in the Greek language: *bios,* a livelihood; *anastrophe,* the behavioral life or lifestyle; *psuche,* self-life; and *zoe,* the life of God. *Anastrophe* is the kind of life which traditional teaching has tried to change, the lifestyle. The only life that will affect the nature of mankind, that will bring a force to truly alter the lifestyle, is *zoe.*

The Word makes it very clear that you are to *keep your heart.* The point is that you have the force that will change your world and those around you. The degree of alteration will be the degree of the working of the force that is in you. We cannot truly change our lives by going to psychiatrists or psychologists, although that can bring some degree of change, but it can never change you to the maximum. Out of the heart flow the life-changing forces. People do not need more religion or tradition. They need the force of zoe, eternal life.

Zoe is the answer to the problem, but the application of the answer has a positive and a negative side. The positive is that within your spirit, as a Christian, is the power to bring healing, deliverance, baptism in the Holy Spirit, salvation, redemption, and the power of God to meet all your needs. Whatever the circumstances, you have within you the power to alter and change them. The negative side is that the power cannot change the situation *unless* it gets out *to* the situation. The thing that hinders the flow of that force is a divided heart. When the heart is not single, the potential for the flow of the forces of life, *zoe,* is greatly diminished.

If any of you lack wisdom, let him ask of God, that giveth to all men liberally, and upbraideth not; and it shall be given him.

But let him ask in faith, nothing wavering. For he that wavereth is like a wave of the sea driven with the wind and tossed.

For let not that man think that he shall receive any thing of the Lord.

A double minded man is unstable in all his ways.

James 1:5-8

The term *"double minded"* in the Greek is *dipsuchos*, which comes from the root *dis-psuche*, or "twice-soulish." It means a split personality, a divided heart. A divided heart occurs when a man's spirit is reaching out in faith and his soul is reaching out in unbelief. Here is a truly divided heart.

The Whole Heart

For years, we have heard the teaching that the heart and the spirit are the same, but that is not correct. The word *heart* in the Greek is *kardia*. The Word *spirit* is *pneuma*. Therefore, the heart is not the spirit, because the original writers of the Bible used the exact words to convey what they meant. The heart is made up of the spirit and soul together. Only the Word, according to Hebrews 4:12, can *merismos*, or divide asunder, the spirit and soul and reveal the core of man. Notice 1 Peter 3:4: But let it be the hidden man of the heart, in that which is not corruptible, even the ornament of a meek and quiet *spirit*, which is in the sight of God of great price.

The hidden man *of* the heart is the spirit man. What would the visible man of the heart be? It would be the soul. Here is why psychiatrists can never bring total and complete help to anyone. They can deal with the *psuche,* soul, to a degree, but they cannot locate or treat the human spirit. Mankind's problems do not just consist of body and soul. Your problem is wrapped up in your heart.

If your heart is divided, you then have dual interests, dual desires, and dual affections. When your heart is divided, you will negate the forces that will change your life and the lives of those around you. If you do not keep your heart, it will not come forth with the forces of life. Remember that to keep it means "to guard it or protect it." What are you guarding your heart against? You are guarding against whatever desires to enter it, because whatever flows in will divide it.

Thou that makest thy boast of the law, through breaking the law dishonourest thou God?

For the name of God is blasphemed among the Gentiles through you, as it is written.

For circumcision verily profiteth, if thou keep the law: but if thou be a breaker of the law, thy circumcision is made uncircumcision.

Therefore if the uncircumcision keep the righteousness of the law, shall not his uncircumcision be counted for circumcision?

And shall not uncircumcision which is by nature, if it fulfil the law, judge thee, who by the letter and circumcision dost transgress the law?

For he is not a Jew, which is one outwardly; neither is that circumcision, which is outward in the flesh:

But he is a Jew, which is one inwardly; and circumcision is that of the heart, in the spirit, and not in the letter; whose praise is not of men, but of God.

Romans 2:23-29

Circumcision is a matter of the heart, in the spirit. With this in mind, let's go to the Book of Ezekiel.

A Stony Heart and a Heart of Flesh

In Ezekiel 36:26 and 27, we will see another example of the difference between heart and spirit. In these verses, we will see clearly what God is saying.

A *new heart* also will I give you, *and* (implying something besides, or in addition to) a *new spirit* will I put within you: and I will take away the stony heart out of your flesh, and I will give you an heart of flesh.

And I will put my spirit within you, and cause you to walk in my statutes, and ye shall keep my judgments, and do them.

The prophet describes two hearts — a stony heart and a heart of flesh. Paul said there would be a circumcision of the heart. What will the circumcision cut away? It will remove the stony heart. In the above verses from Ezekiel, God is saying that He will give us two things: first, a new heart, and second, a new spirit.

We find further insight in Ezekiel 11:19-21.

And I will give them *one heart,* and I will put a new spirit within you; and I will take the stony heart out of their flesh, and will give them an heart of flesh:

That they may walk in my statutes, and keep mine ordinances, and do them: and they shall be my people, and I will be their God.

But as for them whose heart walketh after the heart of their detestable things and their abominations, I will recompense their way upon their own heads, saith the Lord God.

Can your heart follow after detestable things? Yes, it can. That is why you must keep, guard, and preserve it. Jesus said it this way: . . . **for out of the abundance of the heart the mouth speaketh** (Matt. 12:34). James 3:10 tells us: **Out of the same mouth proceedeth blessing and cursing. My brethren, these things ought not so to be.**

From the mouth proceeds sweet water and bitter. If it is going to come from the heart, and the heart is interpreted as the spirit, then we have confusion. The spirit that is born again is born of incorruptible seed and divine nature and cannot sin because it is born of God. Both sweet water and bitter can come out of the heart, but both cannot come out of the spirit. In the divided heart, one side is a heart of flesh and the other side is a stony heart.

The heart of flesh is flexible, pliable, sensitive, easy to work with, under control, and gentle. The other side of the heart is prideful, hard, rebellious, has self-willed tendencies, and is arrogant, boastful, and unmanageable. The stony heart is your behavior or personality. The personality of man is the soulish realm — mind, will, and emotions.

The moment you were born again, your heart became divided because you received a new spirit. Before new birth, your heart and soul were in harmony. At the new birth, however, you began to partake of the spiritual desires of the new nature, and yet, you still had the selfish desires of the soulish man, who was still living like the world. Your spirit was saved instantly, while your soul man is saved progressively. At the new birth, your kingdom became divided against itself — born of the spirit, yet full of selfishness.

We are not dealing with dual natures, but with one nature and two lives: the divine nature in the spirit man and the life of the spirit, *zoe,* as well as the life of the self, *psuche.* Because of that, you have divided interests or desires. For the first few months after being born again, you have a struggle trying to allow the new life to begin flowing. Jesus really wants to begin a work of alignment at that time, taking the newly divided heart and uniting it as one by the saving of the soul so that it can be joined to the spirit — unification for cooperation with one heart, one desire, one effect, and one purpose in God.

Set your affection on things above, not on things on the earth (Col. 3:2). If your spirit affections are on things above while your soulish affections are on things of the earth, you have a divided heart. If you have a divided heart, you must keep your heart with all diligence and preserve it in singleness of mind. Until you do, you will never really change your world or the people around you. The only thing that will bring change is *zoe,* eternal life. The *zoe* of God is in the holy of holies (the spirit), and it will not appear in the outer court (manifestation), unless it passes through the holy place (the soul). Ezekiel says that God will give us one heart.

The Two Hearts

Let's look at the two hearts again for just a moment. Until a person is dealt with, there are interests in his life both toward God *and* away from God, submission to and rebellion toward God. That is why it is so important for you to have a *merismos*, a real work of God in your spirit and soul.

For the first few months after being born again, there is excitement about the things of God, even in the soulish man. You are enjoying the thrill of a new experience, the speaking with tongues of the Spirit-filled life, and the joy of freedom and forgiveness. After a few months go by, and you start hearing the Word on discipline, commitment, faithfulness, and consistency, the soul man starts checking out. Here is where the resistance to the purpose of God begins.

The spirit man's desires are to do the things of God, but the self-life seeks to preserve itself because its desires are still of this world. Here is where the warfare and struggle come in. God wants to bring peace, not through co-existence and compromise, but by bringing a union by process of agreement. **Can two walk together, except they be agreed** (Amos 3:3)?

Jesus is an example of a united heart. His spirit and soul were so harmonized and synchronized that He constantly emanated the *zoe* life of God. Everywhere He went, He healed the sick, raised the dead, cast out devils, cleansed the lepers, and gave words of wisdom and words of knowledge. Everywhere He went and every need that was presented to Him, He met by releasing the *zoe*. Out of His heart came the forces of life.

In Mark 5:25-34, we read the story of the woman who had an issue of blood for twelve years and who had **suffered many things of many physicians** and spent all her money, but was no better. When she came up behind Jesus in the crowd and touched his garment, **she felt in her body that she was healed of that plague. Jesus, immediately knowing in himself that virtue had gone out of him,** turned around and wanted to know who had touched Him!

Did He know who had touched Him? No, but He knew that virtue had gone out of Him. In the light of Proverbs 4:23, we are able to conclude that the issues, the forces, of life had flowed out of Him. Jesus kept His heart in harmony and united at all times. His spiritual and soulish desires were the same.

When you begin to have perplexities, the reason is because of a divided heart. You are out of harmony with the peace and tranquility of God. You have broken the life chain and the forces that emanate life and peace. The moment the soul moves out of harmony with the spirit, you have a divided heart, and you have negated the forces of God's peace, life, and tranquility. The life of God that builds us, and encourages and keeps our faith high, is cut off and your battery begins to discharge. Your spirit man begins to lose his prowess and his potential.

What, then, is the solution? You have to get your heart in unity. The moment your heart comes back into unity, you have a life-giving force from God coming back into you which charges your battery. The more super-charged you are, when you contact the negative post of sickness and disease or any other problem, the more power you will have to release to change it.

In the natural, when a battery has lost power, we call it dead. One of the major things that causes it to be drained is a "short." A short circuit drains the energies, or the life, out of the battery, and there will not be enough of a charge left to meet any demand put on it. What do we do with that battery? We recharge it by hooking it up to a battery charger. Of course, you need to fix the short circuit or the circumstances will be repeated. That is why praying in tongues is so vital.

But ye, beloved, building up yourselves on your most holy faith, praying in the Holy Ghost.

Jude 20

By taking the positive force of *zoe* and hooking up to the negative posts of the soul and body, and by being super-charged by the spirit, we can take the negative out of our body and soul. Through the laying on of hands, you are releasing spirit life into that person to "jumpstart" him and get his engine going.

In the spiritual realm, you must keep the affections and desires of the heart on Jesus, not some on the spirit and some on self. A stony heart will negate the spirit forces.

Breaking Up the Fallow Ground

The key to releasing the spirit man is found in the word *brokenness*. What does brokenness do to a stony heart? It breaks it up. Jeremiah 4:3 says it this way: **For thus saith the Lord to the men of Judah and Jerusalem, break up your fallow ground, and sow not among thorns.** *Fallow ground* is that which has been hardened by exposure to the elements. If you allow your soul to be exposed to the elements for a long period of time and not to the things of Jesus, your soul man will begin to be hardened over. It will become rough, unpliable, and non-responsive to the touch of God.

God was saying through Jeremiah that before He could bring forth the forces of life, He was going to have to bring brokenness to the soul man in order to remove a strength of soul. Once brokenness occurred, the spirit man could have preeminence. People wonder why they aren't healed or don't get their needs met. The answer is that power for change is there, but it is locked up by their soulish realms and negated.

By the time God gets through bringing brokenness to the hard, stony heart, it will be pliable, easily entreated, sensitive to the Spirit of God, and obedient. You will have a good attitude and be submitted to the authority of God and to His authorities in the earth.

In the Tabernacle of the Israelites, the *zoe* was in the Holy of Holies, but it had to pass through the Holy Place to get to the Outer Court where the people were. Our spirit men are our holy of holies, our souls are the holy places between the inner sanctums, and our bodies are the outer courts. The problem is that the glory of God has to go through the channel of the soulish realm in order to reach the body or the physical realm to bring change. The soul will permit it to flow through or stop it, depending on whether the heart is divided or united.

Go back to Amos 3:3: **Can two walk together, except they be agreed?** Can my body, being the temple of God, do the work of God from the spirit when my soul is not in agreement? No, it cannot. This will give more insight into what Jesus meant when He said: **Again I say unto you, That if two of you shall agree on earth as touching any thing that they shall ask, it shall be done for them of my Father which is in heaven** (Matt. 18:19). The Greek word for *agree (sumphoneo)* means "to synchronize."

Jesus wants us to be in agreement in more than just our spirits. Look at Mark 11:23:

> For verily I say unto you, That whosoever shall say unto this mountain, Be thou removed, and be thou cast into the sea; and *shall not doubt in his heart*, but shall believe that those things which he saith shall come to pass; he shall have whatsoever he saith.

It has been said that you can have doubt in your head, but not in your spirit, and receive from God, yet James said that a man who does not ask in faith is a double-minded man. The reason you're not having what you're saying is because you are doubting in your heart. The word *doubt* in the Greek is *diakrino* and is from two words: *dia*, which means "a channel through which something else flows," and *krino*, which means "to distinguish, to decide, to hesitate." *Diakrino* is a channel through which you hesitate or are uncertain or unsure. If I have a hesitation about what I am saying, will I receive it? No, I will not.

In other words, if my spirit and my soul are not walking together in agreement, my receiving will be hindered. If they can get together as touching the thing for which I am believing, however, it will be done. You *can* have what you say.

"Unite My Heart"

Does God want to unite our hearts? Yes, He does, because when our hearts are divided, we are disunited. We are not in agreement with ourselves. It is only when my spirit and soul have the same desires and aspirations that my heart is united. As I keep it preserved to be sure that nothing alien creeps in and vies for the attention of my desires, out of my innermost being shall

214

flow rivers of living water that people can drink to change their lives and affect their destinies.

Teach me thy way, O Lord; I will walk in thy truth: *unite my heart* **to fear thy name.**

Psalm 86:11

I want my heart to be united so that I may fear His name. I will fear missing God because my heart and my affections are on Him. My spirit and soul *are* turned toward Him.

For the life of God to reach the Body, it must come *from* the spirit *through* the soul. Now you can see why some get healing and some do not. I have laid hands on people and felt that virtue go out of me into them and come right back into my body. Why? The virtue was directed toward the body and toward a receptive spirit, but the person's heart was divided so that when the virtue, or the power from the Holy Spirit, hit the soul, it was not permitted to flow to the body. It returned to the channel from which it came.

15

THE RELEASE OF THE SPIRIT

Zoe is a force. It is the life of God. We have already seen that this force is what alters and changes everything. For the law of the spirit of life in Christ Jesus hath made me free from the law of sin and death (Rom. 8:2). This law of *zoe* is a law of the spirit.

> My son, attend to my words; incline thine ear unto my sayings.
>
> Let them not depart from thine eyes; keep them in the midst of thine heart.
>
> For they are life unto those that find them, and health to all their flesh.
>
> Keep thy heart with all diligence; for out of it are the issues of life.
>
> Proverbs 4:20-23

The thing the spirit man looks for is that which produces life. Once the spirit man finds that, he wants to hook-up with it. One of the reasons why people are not satisfied with where they are is because they have not found life. They look to find it, and wherever life is being produced, those who have life, or are looking for life, will go there.

It is out of the heart that the forces of life flow. From the spirit man, through the soul, flows the *zoe*. By the spirit, we are able to measure others. When a spirit-dominated person meets other people, he is able to measure their spiritual prowess and depth in order to see what spiritual level they are on. The problem, however, is that with most people, we never touch their spirits, only the strengths of their personality or *psuche* life.

The strengths of the soul often are referred to in the natural world as weaknesses, but they are *not* weaknesses. The inferiority complex is one of the greatest strengths of *psuche*, and yet it has been classified as a weakness. Regardless of what complex may be involved, being a part of your personality or self-life, it will dictate your behavior. Pride, arrogance, and haughtiness all come from the soulish realm. When we make contact, very often those areas are the ones that must be dealt with before the spirit force can even be tapped.

One cannot fellowship with that person because a *pneumatikos* man cannot fellowship with a *psuchikos* man. The only fellowship we have is described in 1 John 1:3: **And truly our fellowship is with the Father, and with His son Jesus Christ.** God is a *spirit.* He uses a spiritual principle through which we can fellowship with Him, and that is the law of the spirit of *zoe.* The life of God has enabled me to fellowship the Father on His level, a spiritual realm, with life.

What must be brought about is an alteration. We must be able to tap in with our spirit man to bring forth to other people the forces of life. Let us look at some things that help us release our spirit man. Remember, the spirit man has the most powerful force in this world. Why? The spirit man can size up every person. He can size up the thoughts and intents of the heart. He is able to measure space, span, and distance. His limitations depend on the strengths of the soul. The degree of your spiritual prowess will be equal to the degree of your soul strengths (weaknesses, in reality). Spiritual prowess cannot exceed the limits of the soul, in other words. If your soul man has been greatly dealt with by God, then your spirit man is released and thankful for his freedom and liberty.

Jesus said in John 6:63: **It is the spirit that quickeneth; the flesh profiteth nothing: the words that I speak unto you, they are spirit** (*pneuma*), **and they are life** (*zoe*). Jesus was saying that the spirit gives life. Your spirit has the forces to bring life to others. If you try to give life from the soul, however, you give the *psuche*, self-life, a lifestyle of self-interests, self-indulgence, and self-pursuit. People are trying to live life that way. That is the thrust of emphasis on mind education and body exercise. They are trying to produce what man desires by the avenues they know.

If you are dualistic in concept, soul and body are the only avenues you know. What is the problem? Flesh profiteth nothing. You can be highly intelligent and still go to hell. You can be muscle-bound and still go to hell. It is the spirit that quickeneth or makes alive. When we learn this, we put less security in natural talents, our own abilities, our own wisdom, or anything else of soul or body. It is the releasing of the forces of life through the spirit of man that profits in life.

Jesus said in Matthew 12:34 that from the abundance of the heart, the mouth speaks. We have to learn how to speak the Word of God. Those are the words that are spirit and life. Learn to speak words that are spiritual and give life. If you are able to do that, it will bring change.

The Candle of the Lord

Proverbs 20:27 says that **the spirit of man is the candle of the Lord, searching all the inward parts of** the belly. Here we see that the spirit is the candle of the Lord. A better translation is that the spirit of man is the *lamp* of the Lord. With that in mind, look at Psalm 18:28: **For thou wilt light my candle: the Lord my God will enlighten my darkness.** When does God "light your candle." It is lit when you are born again. The moment you confessed, "Jesus is Lord" and received Him, your candle, your spirit man, was lit. You became spiritually alive.

When the spirit becomes God's candle, He uses it to *search* with. What is He searching? He searches the *inward* parts of the belly (Prov. 20:27).

> But as it is written, Eye hath not seen, nor ear heard, neither have entered into the heart of man, the things which God hath prepared for them that love him.

> 1 Corinthians 2:9

The above verse is the way it was before you were born again, but verse 10 goes on to say: **But God hath revealed them unto us by his Spirit.** What is the *them* that He has revealed? **Those things which God hath prepared for them that love him.** God revealed them to us by His Spirit: **for the Spirit *searcheth* all things, yea, the deep things of God** (1 Cor. 2:10). The Spirit searches the deep things of God, but what does the candle or lamp search? It searches the inward parts of the belly.

For what man knoweth the things of a man, save the spirit of man which is in him? (Paul is saying, "Who can know the things of me but my spirit?") **even so the things of God knoweth no man, but the Spirit of God** (1 Cor. 2:11). The spirit of man cannot know the things of God apart from the Spirit of God. It is the Holy Spirit who searches them out to reveal to the spirit man.

Once your spirit is born again, God takes the things of Himself and illuminates the inward parts. The spirit, soul, and body then can know what is available from God. Psalm 42:7 says it this way: **Deep calleth unto deep.** That means that it is the Spirit of God searching all the deep things of God and the things He finds there, **deep calleth unto deep.** The Spirit of God calls to the spirit of man by using him as a candle so that the deep things of God can be revealed to the depths of man.

We can then supersede all reasonings and intellect. That was why the Pharisees thought Jesus was crazy. He was the only one right in a world of wrong. Why was this so? Jesus superseded the intellect of man and went into the deep things of God by His spirit. His spirit man, cooperating with the Spirit of God, was searching out the deep things of God. The Spirit of God, cooperating with the spirit man, was searching out the deep things of man. The result was the fulfilling of 1 Corinthians 2:12-16.

> **Now we have received, not the spirit of the world, but the spirit which is of God;** *that we might know the things that are freely given to us of God.* (That we might know!)
>
> **Which things also we speak, not in the words which man's wisdom teacheth, but which the Holy Ghost teacheth; comparing spiritual things with spiritual.**
>
> **But the natural man receiveth not the things of the Spirit of God: for they are foolishness**

unto him: *neither can he know them,* because they are spiritually discerned.

But he that is spiritual judgeth all things, yet he himself is judged of no man.

For who hath known the mind of the Lord, that he may instruct him? But we have the mind of Christ.

Here is what is being said: The soul of man and the Spirit of God are irreconcilable, but once the spirit man is born again, he becomes lit and the Spirit of God searches all the things of God. My spirit man searches all the inward parts of the belly so that I can know two things in my life in order to function properly. I can know the things of God and *I can know the things of myself. We have put the most emphasis on searching out the things of God, yet God wants us to search out the things of our lives as well. He wants us to reveal and unveil the things of the soulish lifestyle so that He can change and alter it.*

Apart from the Spirit of God and the spirit of man, all anyone can do is pluck the fruit but never deal with the root. We want to sever the root system and deal with the problems successfully and, to do this, you must keep your heart unified, because out of it flow the issues, the forces of zoe. Look at 1 Corinthians 2:10. The deep things of God reveal the very core or center of the Father Himself.

Proverbs 20:27 tells us that the Spirit of God wants to use the spirit man to search out the very core of man, the hidden parts. We are not to adorn our exterior with just the things of gold, with clothing, and all this sort of thing. We are told to be adorned by the hidden man of the heart, the spirit man, but there is another man of the heart that is not hidden, the soul or the personality of man. The Spirit of God has, through the years, used my spirit man as a flashlight to reveal the ways of truth and reveal myself to me until I understood what it means to truly be a "triune man."

I have learned the ways of Randy's personality, and the ways of Randy's spirit man. These two ways have not always cooperated with the ways of God. I have had to take the life of God and begin to bring about alterations in the soul man so that what I received would be able to line up with what I discovered in the depths of God. Deep calls unto deep, and they must align themselves properly.

Division and Brokenness

There is a two-fold work of God that takes place in your life. This is the work of "division" and "brokenness," and this is the way of *zoe.* Division is the first step. During the division stage, God's Word, being quick and powerful, separates the spirit and soul of a man and divides, not detaches, them for clarification so that you can understand about your spirit, *zoe,* and about your soul, *psuche.* The division is between spiritual and natural forces, between spiritual and natural abilities, and between spiritual and natural talents.

You can tell when the distinction has not been made, because God gets little done through the person who is so strong in his own intellect, natural abilities, and talents. One example is in the area of musical ability. You can learn to play a piano, yet not bring life to it. It is merely natural ability. There needs to be a distinction, or *merismos,* made. The area in which division will work most is in the heart, which is made up of your spirit and soul.

In this division, we have to make a real clarification because God said that every kingdom divided against itself will fall. Every house divided will come to desolation. The heart divided will not bring success and life. Your spirit and soul cannot walk together except they be in agreement. You cannot agree until you come into harmony. Once the division has come to bring distinction, then the second area, brokenness, must come into play.

When the soulish strengths, attributes, potentials, and strongholds begin to be revealed, it is the revelation of a stony heart or fallow ground, both hard and unreceptive. God begins to deal with us in order to eventually unite us and give us one heart, not a divided heart. The major way in which He does this is by bringing brokenness to us, by breaking up the fallow ground.

Brokenness is the tempering and taming, by the Spirit of God, of the soul man so that he is no longer hard but has become pliable and flexible. He becomes cooperative, sensitive, and submissive to the Spirit of God.

Why is it that when God begins to probe your life you become offended? One of the purposes of fasting is: **And that thou hide not thyself from thine own flesh** (Isa. 58:7). The soul man starts rising up, and you get angry or irritated. Fasting strengthens your spirit and provokes your soul, so that he is very much on display.

Why do people never seem to maintain the blessings of God and only partake spasmodically of the moves of God? The reason is that the spirit man is only permitted freedom spasmodically. A stony heart, known as the soulish lifestyle, keeps the spirit from being released. The soulish lifestyle is full of "I don't think that is of God, I don't believe tongues are for today, I don't feel healed, and so forth." Disbelief and criticism are areas of resistance to the forces of life. The stony heart will not allow the joy and pleasure of the life of the spirit. When the soul refuses to cooperate with the forces of *zoe*, immediately the joy, life, and victory of that person is tampered with.

Our source of fellowship is in meeting spirit to spirit. Our own insecurities, which need to be dealt with as strengths of the soul, keep us from having the right fellowship with one another. Unbelief, insecurity, intimidation, and hardness of heart stop the life of the spirit.

Jesus said, **By their fruits ye shall know them** (Matt. 7:20). We should be able to recognize when we move out of the spirit into the soul by the fruit the change produces. It takes joy and life from you, and you start thinking weird, and doing strange things. Stupid decisions are made in a state like that. You will walk away from a move of God thinking you don't belong there, but it was your own hardness of heart that separated you from that move. If your heart had been broken up, your spirit man would have shed a light on the situation, revealed the truth, and uncovered the lies and wrong thinking.

We must cease from partaking of the Tree of Knowledge of Good and Evil. We must partake of the Tree of Life. In the day that you partake of the wrong tree, your spirit man suffers. The life of God is once again held in bondage with the spirit man unable to be released. The real you is the spirit man who is being held prisoner by the soul. It is in the spirit that reside the attributes of God — life, light, and love.

Life Reproduces Light

Zoe life will always reproduce illumination or light. Look at the following scriptures:

In him was life; and the life was the light of men (John 1:4); **It is the spirit that quickeneth; the flesh profiteth nothing: the words that I speak unto you, they are spirit, and they are life** (John 6:63); **Thy word is a lamp unto my feet, and a light unto my path** (Ps. 119:105); and, The entrance of thy words giveth light; it giveth understanding unto the simple (Ps. 119:130).

Zoe produces illumination, comprehension, understanding, wisdom, and knowledge, because in life abides light. The illumination to mankind is the light of God's Word, and His Words are spirit and life. They feed the spirit man and bring insight to the whole of man. Once the work of brokenness is done and the heart is realigned, you become the most powerful force in the earth.

There are two types of Christians. One has the life of God restricted and imprisoned. *Zoe* is not able to function. It has been received, but is all wrapped up by the power of self. *Zoe* cannot come forth because they are not *keeping* their hearts against that type of thing. Therefore, they are unable to emanate life to others. These people are depressed, frustrated, unhappy, defeated, angry, critical, judgmental, backbiters, and gossipers. Everything that comes out of them is death. They are bringing forth that which comes from themselves.

If you judge someone else, you are judging them of, or from, yourself. If you judge from your soul, that also is the way you are judged. **Judge not, that ye be** not judged. **For with what judgment ye judge, ye shall be judged** (Matt. 7:1).

The other type of Christian is the one who has finally learned how to release the life of God. Through the work of brokenness, he has gotten rid of the hardness of heart in order to allow the *zoe* to pour forth. That is the goal, and it is an attainable goal. By division and brokenness, God is going to bring us into a revelation of ourselves so that His life can come forth at any time. God can cause you to locate your place in the Body so that you may function and fulfill your part. We want to see, not just the negatives, but the positives. We want to see your calling, election, selection, potential, and ability to truly be all that God made you to be. All this must flow from a united heart.

16
BEAUTY IN BROKENNESS

You can develop sensitivity to God through the beauty of brokenness. I want to share out of my heart on this subject. One of the greatest needs in the lives of Christians is the ability to develop a brokenness within the heart. We will then become sensitive to God, to His Spirit, and to the needs of people. Very few Christians have developed the ability to size up other people in order to help them, to understand where they are coming from, what they are experiencing, what their frustrations, pains, and troubles are, and to be able to help them. The Church has been so "surface" and shallow, it is pathetic.

The reason for this lack of sensitivity is that we are too much concerned with our own world and our own problems. You will never be sensitive and broken enough to deal with others until your selfishness has been extracted from you, and your own "world" is of less importance than someone else's.

Jesus saith unto them, did ye never read in the scriptures, The stone which the builders rejected, the same is become the head of the corner: this is the Lord's doing, and it is marvellous in our eyes?

Therefore say I unto you, The kingdom of God shall be taken from you, and given to a nation bringing forth the fruits thereof.

And whosoever shall fall on this stone shall be broken: but on whomsoever it shall fall, it will grind him to powder.

Matthew 21:42-44

My wife and I have experienced many times the work of a sensitive heart. As we have been eating in restaurants, I have known by the Spirit what certain people had been praying about and what their situation was at that moment. At times, He would even give me the names of some of them. As a result, I was able to minister to their needs, to sit at their table and share from my heart what the Holy Spirit had told me about them.

Wherever you may be, there are people with needs. Many of them are God's children, and His eye is upon them. (2 Chron. 16:9.) The problem is that Christianity and ministry are "building oriented." If the situation does not present itself within the confines of our traditional way of thinking, we will not release the Spirit. Some Christians have been so encrusted and hard that God could drop a rock on them, and they wouldn't feel it. They are insensitive to any touch of God.

There is a place where, once we have been dealt with by God and once His breath comes, we instantly respond. His breath is not a turbulent wind, but a still, small voice which moves upon our spirits many times a day to bring insight, direction, and wisdom. Always be aware, however, that insensitivity will not permit response.

Jesus perfected this in his earth walk. He cultivated fellowship with the Father. His sensitivity was so great that He could perceive the thoughts and intents of the hearts of men. He could read lives as if He were reading off a piece of paper with detailed accuracy. He always picked up on the hurts of people, so much so that He identified with them. His sensitivity is seen in the instance where He was aware of virtue having gone out of Him by the touch of faith. He was constantly aware of His surroundings and the situations about Him. His world was one of total awareness of His purpose. The purpose of God is His people. Jesus said to me, "My presence brings My power, My power brings My purpose, and My purpose is My people."

Being aware of those around you comes as a result of developing the spirit man and brokenness. Brokenness is the strengthening of the spirit man and the weakening of the soul. It is dealing with the heart of man. **Behold, thou desirest truth in the inward parts: and in the hidden part thou shalt make me to know wisdom** (Ps. 51:6). God desires to bring truth to the hidden parts of man, his spirit and soul.

God's Spirit uses my spirit as a flashlight to reveal and make me known to myself. The joy of knowing that is that my spirit man will not excuse me. He is constantly shining upon me to get me corrected, instructed, and reproved, so that I can remove myself from the judgment and condemnation of the world. My spirit man will not allow the soul man to operate independently of God.

The divine nature of God is made up of life, light, and love. These three characteristics are the keys to bringing us to a place of successfully dealing with other people. God's life, *zoe*, is what we must learn to release to others, and that life released will bring light. (John 1:4.) By being able to release life, we also will be able to walk in illumination and comprehension, understanding God's dealings in our lives. One thing that has amazed me is that as God begins to deal with me about an individual, and I respond by going to them, I always find that He has already been dealing with them Himself in that area. Through these dealings, we are able to come into the purpose of God.

The Sacrifice of Brokenness

Brokenness, in its Biblical context, has been greatly misunderstood. In dealing with it, the Church has related it too much to the breaking of horses, in a wrong way. Psalm 51:10 says: **Create in me a clean heart, O God; and renew a right spirit within me.** The 17th verse reads: **The sacrifices of God are a broken spirit: a broken and a contrite heart, O God, thou wilt not despise.**

A horse has no spirit. It is dualistic — body and soul. Mankind is the only part of creation that has a spirit, and spirit is to rule soul. Soul cannot rule soul. There is no authority in the soul. That is why people who try to rule from their souls use intimidation, manipulation, and exploitation as the means to achieve their ends. Because of misunderstanding "breaking the spirit" of an animal, we are confused about brokenness in us. What is really broken in that animal? The strength of its will is broken. If you *train* it, you don't have to *break* it!

The use of force and brutality is not the way of God. The idea of breaking as the product of impatience is *not* what I'm talking about. We need to understand brokenness in another sense. Brokenness is not God breaking your will, although there will come brokenness to the will. In looking at Psalm 51:17, keep in mind that the heart is more than the spirit. The psalmist is showing us how to have a sensitivity of heart. To do this, the entire heart has to be dealt with, spirit and soul.

Remember, the continual two-fold work of God in your life is division and brokenness. All of your life, you will experience that which is from your spirit and that which is from self that you thought was of the spirit! God will deal with you through brokenness every time He brings a division between your spirit and soul in order to expose a wrong area of your soul.

Breaking Up the Fallow Ground

We discussed this aspect earlier, in Chapter 14. Remember the passage from Jeremiah 4:3,4 concerning the breaking up of the fallow, hardened, crusted-over ground, and the verses in Ezekiel concerning God's replacing a stony heart with a heart of flesh? God wants to give us a new spirit *and* a new heart of flesh, a two-fold working of God to bring about one heart. Ground that has been lying exposed to the elements is not productive, nor ready to receive seed until it has been broken up.

In Mark 4:14-20, four types of ground are described but only one type of seed. The problem in reproducing fruit is not in the seed, but in the ground. There is only one seed, which is the Word, but four ways to receive it. That is why not everyone who hears the Word is producing to the fullest potential. The reason is a ground problem. Their ground is not reproducing fruit. There is great frustration in needing to eat of God's fruit, but when you reach for it, it is not there. You constantly go to your ground to partake of the fruit, and there is nothing there. You must find out what is happening.

The four types of ground were described by Jesus as: *the wayside, stony ground, thorns, and good ground.* All Christians think they are good ground, but Jeremiah says to break up the fallow ground and not sow among thorns. That applies to the people of God.

To understand the operation of this, we need to look at the ministry of John the Baptist, called the *plowman ministry.* At times, praise and worship is used as a plowman ministry. At other times, we can see this ministry through the manifestations of the Spirit. The strongest plowman on the earth today, however, is a real prophet of God. Why is he needed? He is needed in order to break up the fallow, hard ground and to bring disruption into the lives of those who think they have it so together but really are lackadaisical and comfortable.

Plows do that to settled ground. They are for the purpose of turning over the soil. You need to be continually exposed to the *plowman ministry.* The prophet will challenge you in the areas where you are not producing fruit. He will move you out of the "satisfied" lifestyle. God wants to plow us up so that we can receive the seed that will bring forth fruit. They took off the head of John the Baptist, but they couldn't take his ministry. It is still in the earth today.

Brokenness is a major aspect of God. Oh, yes, you can avoid it, just as you can avoid being born again. Even though it is God's will that none perish (2 Pet. 3:9), many do. Because of their hardness of heart, the truth of God cannot be revealed in their inward parts. When you get into the Word and revelation starts to come, your mind will rise up and contradict it with reason and logic, if the soul is in control. All of a sudden, that seed is taken out of your heart and no longer reproduces in you. The "fowl" just robbed you of that seed, and one day, you'll go looking for a harvest and there will be none.

If the soil has been greatly dealt with by God, it is beautiful, tenderized, and sensitized soil that has been sifted and absorbed. It is real soft. You can take a seed of any size, throw it into that soil, and it will grow. The principle of reproduction is that the soil must receive the seed before it can bring forth. Because of the hardness in the different areas of people's hearts, many times God is not able to bring forth His best in them.

We have been taught to believe in Jesus as Savior, Healer, and Provider, but all that is directed to each person, individually. We need to become sensitized enough to direct the forces of His life to others whenever we are moved with compassion and whenever we are easily touched by the feeling of their infirmities. Brokenness is for no other reason than to bring a tameness to the soul man so that he will be sensitive to the leading of God's Spirit in ministry to others.

Brokenness — Tamed to Obedience

I have taken all the scriptures I know and begun to use them on my horses, who are dualistic — soul and body. With the firstborn, from the moment of his birth, I touched him, loved him, and, yes, brought correction to him, but never by fear or rejection. I spent weeks with him, and now I can go out anywhere in the pasture and call his name, and he will come right up to me. It is not so with the other two. They run away when I start toward them. The reason is that the second horse was about six years old when I bought her and already "programmed," and when the third came, I hardly had any time to work with her. What made the difference? One had the attention, the others did not. I neglected to oversee the soul of the third horse and left her to herself. You cannot leave the soul without spiritual authority. Remember that there is no authority from the soul. It must come from the spirit. A horse broken by impatience will only respond to the harshness of the rider. A trained horse will respond to a gentle tug, having developed sensitivity to the reins.

The rod and reproof give wisdom: but a child left to himself bringeth his mother to shame (Prov. 29:15). Now we understand why our children go to public schools and come out rebellious. There is no spiritual authority there anymore. It is just soul versus soul. Children today are not respecting authority, because they are not perceiving any authority.

We are to be the meek, the sensitive of spirit, those who have come under submission and control of the Holy Spirit because of being dealt with so much in the soulish realm that, when God makes a turn, you almost instantly respond to His gentle tug on the reins of your heart.

People wonder why tragedy happens to Christians. One of the big reasons is that we have not become sensitive to the leading of the Spirit, and we will not, until we learn the work of brokenness in our lives. People say, "It's so hard." No, it's only hard on the soul. The spirit man loves it. **The preparations of the heart in man, and the answer of the tongue, is from the Lord** (Prov. 16:1). Does God want to bring preparation before you speak? Of course, He does, but the untamed soul likes to speak its mind and to express views and opinions. On the other hand, the spirit man wants to wait upon God for what to speak. From now on, allow your preparation to come from the Lord, so that when you speak, you will speak for Him.

Matthew 21:44 says **And whosoever shall fall on this stone shall be broken: but on whomsoever it shall fall, it will grind him to powder.** That is a true statement. Brokenness deals with taking away the strength of your will. The old theological interpretation of "God, break my will" is not correct as it has been presented. People have thought God was just going to take them and *make* them do what He wanted. No, He will only break your will, when you *will* to be broken, or when you *will* to fall upon the Stone.

Take your life and lay it on the Rock. When God brings brokenness, you will be able to release the life of the spirit through a heart of flesh — one that has been broken and weakened by the Spirit of God, is inclined to the will of God, and is ready to wait for the Spirit to initiate action. A heart of flesh is not going to do anything until the Spirit of God tells him what to do. No more of the spirit man having to run down the soul, rope him and jump on his back, and rein back tightly on him, trying to get him under control.

God refers to the soul of man as *Esau*, which means "wild ass," a stubborn, rebellious donkey. You say, "Oh, no, not *me*, God!" If not you, then let's see you bring forth the hundredfold fruit, or maybe even the sixty-fold. It is time to take a real good look at our ground. We must get into the area where we have been dealt with by God, the area that has experienced a *merismos* and a brokenness. Those who have experienced the working of God's Spirit in their lives are meek people, easily entreated, sensitive, not talkative, arrogant, boastful, and opinionated. They are slow to speak, not pushing personality, but transparent. Their spirits can be touched and can touch others. We realize that the treasure is not the earthen vessel, but the treasure is Christ which is in the earthen vessel. The flesh profiteth nothing.

Before and After Brokenness

There are two distinct conditions to be seen in those who possess the work of *zoe* through their lives. There are those whose spirits have forged their way through the outer shells and brought forth, and those in whom the *zoe* is still confined, restricted, and imprisoned. Brokenness deals with the breaking of the outer shell.

Everything God does is based on the principle of the life of *zoe*. We can see the work of brokenness in a single natural illustration. You will not drink orange juice until you break the outer part of the fruit and squeeze. You won't drink apple juice until you squeeze and bring forth the juice. What did Jesus do with the bread when feeding the multitudes? (Matt. 14:19.) He broke it before He could distribute it. He cannot distribute us until there is brokenness. We are to become broken bread and poured out wine.

You will never become broken until you fall upon the Rock and say, "God, in the name of Jesus, take Your mighty hand and work brokenness within me. I want to be broken by the hand of the Master. Take out of me resistance, anger, and hostility. Take out of me arrogance, haughtiness, and pride. Take out of me those things that are my opinions, views, and ideas. Make me something in the hands of the Master so that You can take me, break me, and distribute me to people in need."

Brokenness removes the hardness, rebellion, resistance, and independence, and produces tenderness, obedience, submission, and dependence. God did not put us in this world to be ministered unto, but to minister, to give the same life that Jesus gave, to lay down our *psuche,* our self-life. God did not call me to build my kingdom. He called me to help establish His that is already built and to see that Jesus Christ is glorifed. God does not want to distribute day-old bread. That is why He told the Israelites to gather up fresh each morning what He had for them that day and not live off yesterday's bread.

God wants us to have a broken and contrite heart. *Contrite* means "to be humble or quick to repent." That is what God wants us to have, a heart that is quick to repent, sensitive, quick to turn and quick to say, "I'm sorry. Thank you for correcting me." Psalm 34:18 says that He is nigh those who have broken hearts and saves those with contrite spirits.

There are people to whom you are close, and others that you are far from because you don't know them well. For the same reason, God is close to those who have broken hearts. The more I know you and the more the walls are broken down between us, the more I can trust you, and the closer we become. Those who do not have broken hearts are not close to God. I'm not talking about space or distance, but about fellowship and relationship. He is speaking, yet you do not hear. That is not closeness. What caused it? Your hardness of heart.

He is there with you all the time, but do you know that He is there? Are you aware of His presence? If not, fall on the Rock and be broken. Can I dwell in a high and holy place with God? (Isa. 57:15.) Yes, but only if

I have a broken and contrite heart, then He and I can have a fellowship that supersedes nominal Christianity. When I am broken and all the dirt clods have become soft, and He breathes upon me, I will perceive His breath. He doesn't have to pull and tug at the reins. My soul has learned to wait for God to speak to the spirit man and move in cooperation with the spirit.

Before Brokenness

Before brokenness, your spirit man is inert, subdued, unstirred, and unable to express himself. He is unable to function. He is confined, restricted, and imprisoned. Even when he does come forth, it is in a mixture of soulish thoughts and strengths, and the result is confusing. Many have done that in prophesying. They began in the Spirit and ended in self. God is not near you if you do that. You've gone on down the road without Him. The soul man is energized by his own strengths and is reluctant, resistant, and uncooperative when the spirit man is stirred. The outer does not obey the dictates of the inner. This is the position of the Body of Christ most of the time.

After Brokenness

After brokenness, the spirit man has come through and is confident, bold, and strong. His main attribute is the presence of God. The soul man is subdued and has become the yielded vessel. He does what you do when you come to a "yield" sign: he yields the right of way. He no longer lives an independent life. He considers others and is quiet, calm, and relaxed. He has entered his rest and is cooperative and supportive of the spirit man. He is tamed to obedience. The outer now obeys the dictates of the inner.

You can be a dynamic man or woman of God if you will lay hold of the teaching in this book. Your spirit and soul will come into agreement. Your spirit man is precious in the sight of God. Your soul will have submitted, and you now will have one heart. When the spirit and soul are in agreement, they work together to fulfill the will of God on the Earth as they were supposed to do. They are quick to react to the Spirit of God.

Brokenness releases the spirit and brings forth the forces of life. It is the unleashing of spiritual prowess and ability. Brokenness reverses the roles of spirit and soul. After brokenness, the spirit man is the man of preeminence.